CAREERS FOR

BOOKWORMS
& Other
Literary Types

VGM Careers for You Series

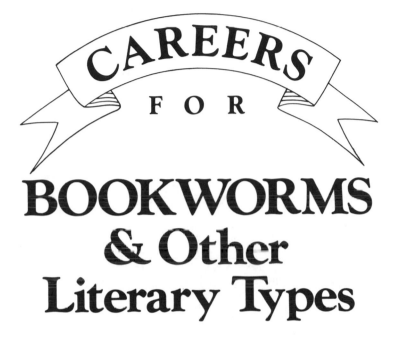

CAREERS FOR

BOOKWORMS
& Other
Literary Types

Second Edition

Marjorie Eberts
Margaret Gisler

VGM Career Horizons
a division of *NTC Publishing Group*
Lincolnwood, Illinois USA

Dedication

To Patty White, our favorite bookworm, who reads books, hoards books, and keeps them as friends forever.

Library of Congress Cataloging-in-Publication Data

Eberts, Marjorie.
  Careers for bookworms & other literary types / Marjorie Eberts,
Margaret Gisler.
      p.   cm.—(VGM careers for you series)
  Includes bibliographical references.
  ISBN 0-8442-4335-3 (h).—ISBN 0-8442-4336-1 (s)
    1. Book industries and trade—Vocational guidance—United States.
  2. Publishers and publishing—Vocational guidance—United States.
  3. Information science—Vocational guidance—United States.
  4. Library science—Vocational guidance—United States.
  5. Research—Vocational guidance—United States.   I. Gisler,
Margaret.   II. Title.   III. Title: Careers for bookworms and other
literary types.   IV. Series.
  Z471.E25   1995
  3818.450028023—dc20   95-3219
                                                                              CIP

1996 Printing

Published by VGM Career Horizons, a division of NTC Publishing Group
4255 West Touhy Avenue
Lincolnwood (Chicago), Illinois 60646-1975, U.S.A.
© 1995 by NTC Publishing Group. All rights reserved.
No part of this book may be reproduced, stored in a retrieval system,
or transmitted in any form or by any means,
electronic, mechanical, photocopying, recording or otherwise,
without the prior permission of NTC Publishing Group.
Manufactured in the United States of America.

  6 7 8 9 0 VP 9 8 7 6 5 4 3 2

Contents

About the Authors

Marjorie Eberts and Margaret Gisler have been writing professionally for 16 years. They are prolific free-lance authors with more than fifty books in print. Their writing is concentrated in the field of education. The two authors have written textbooks, beginning readers, and study skills books for schoolchildren. They have also written a speech book for adults, numerous career books, a college preparation handbook, and several books designed to help parents guide their children through school.

Besides writing books, the two authors have a syndicated education column, "Dear Teacher," which appears in newspapers throughout the country. Eberts and Gisler also give advice on educational issues in speeches, at workshops, and on television.

Writing this book was a special pleasure for Eberts and Gisler because they are decidedly bookworms. Investigating the many careers that require reading on-the-job let them spend hours reading—their favorite avocation and an essential part of their work.

Eberts is a graduate of Stanford University, and Gisler is a graduate of Ball State and Butler Universities. Both received their specialist degrees in education from Butler University. The two authors also have more than 20 years of teaching experience between them.

Acknowledgments

Some bookworms have jobs that let them spend considerable time reading. We would especially like to thank the following dedicated bookworms for providing us with career information.

KATHY BARNARD	Indianapolis-Marion County Public Library
SUE ELLEN BLOMBERG	Howard J. Rubenstein Associates
ROGER BROOKS	Legislative Auditor's Office, Minnesota
L. T. BROWN	*Indianapolis News*
STEVE BUSHOUSE	Butler University
CHRIS CAIRO	Indianapolis-Marion County Public Library
BILL CARNES	United States Army Finance Corps
MARGARET CARNEY	Harlequin Books
AL CARP	International Multifoods
BETSY CAUFIELD	*Indianabolis Star and News*
BILL CHRISTOPHERSEN	*Newsweek*
THOMAS COCHRUN	WTHR, Indianapolis
PATRICK COLEMAN	Minnesota Historical Society
HELEN M. CORRALES	Hoover Institution
ELIZABETH CRAWFORD	Indianapolis-Marion County Public Library
WILLIAM DEJOHN	University of Minnesota
JENNIE DUFFY	Diablo Publications
DON ELLER	Mosely Securities Corporation
JOHN W. ELLWOOD	University of Minnesota
SUE ENGLEDOW	Clay Junior High School

SANDY ERICKSON	Vick Ramos
TIM ERICKSON	University of Wisconsin
SARA EVANS	University of Minnesota
JACQUELINE FISCHER	Indianapolis-Marion County Public Library
SANDY FITZGERALD	*Indianapolis Star and News*
JUDY GALBRAITH	Free Spirit
DENECE GILBERT	
CHERYL GRAHAM	World Book
VALISKA GREGORY	Free-Lance Book Reviewer
STANLEY GREIGG	Congressional Budget Office
FRED GRISSONI	American Printing House for the Blind
FRAN HAGEBOECK	Mohawk Trails Elementary School
DAWN HALL	*Indianapolis Star and News*
BETH HARRIS	Associated Press
DENNIS HETZEL	*The Daily Record*
PATRICIA HOLT	National Book Critics Circle
DEIDRE HOUCEK	Marketing Research Corporation of America
RHONDA HUNNICUTT	Carmel Clay Public Library
KAREN ZACK INGEBRETSEN	World Book
JAYE ISLER	Author
DALE JACOBS	World Book
JOAN JOHNSTON	Stanford University
DEBORAH JONES	Hudson Institute
JACK HUGHES	Mosely Securities Coporation
FELICE KNARR	Roncalli High School
GREG KNIPE	Walden Books
FRANK KNOUREK	General Mills
RANDY KORNFIELD	MGM
VALERIE KOUTNIK	Screenwriter
CYNTHIA KROOS	Villa Holidays
JOHN LEVINE	Dorsey and Whitney
MATT LEVY	
DAVID MACANALLY	WTHR, Indianapolis
BARBARA EVANS MARKUSON	Indiana Cooperative Library Services Authority
KAREN MCCALL	Oakley School
SHIRLEY MULLIN	Kids Ink

MARGARET MYERS	American Library Association
ROBERT NELSON	The Lilly Laboratory for Clinical Research
TERRI NELSON	International Multifoods
MOLLY PARSONS	A.C. Nielsen
JANET PETERSON	World Book
JEFF PIGEON	WIBC, Indianapolis
DAVID PROFELSKI	World Book
BOBBIE REEVES	The American Society of Indexers
STEVE RIES	Barnes and Thornburg
PAUL RHUNQUIST	Library of Congress
JILL SANSONE	Book of the Month Club
JULIE G. SEDKY	Capital Insights Group
EVELYN SIMPSON	Carmel Clay Public Library
PATTY STANTON	KGO, San Francisco
BILL WEPLER	Indiana State Museum
HERBERT S. WHITE	Indiana University
JOHN WILLIAMS	House Research Department, Minnesota
RONALD WILSON	*Newsweek*
DAVE WOOD	*Minneapolis Star Tribune*

CHAPTER ONE

A Look at Careers for Bookworms

On July 10, 1815, Thomas Jefferson wrote in a letter to John Adams, "I cannot live without books." This expresses perfectly the philosophy of all true bookworms. The lives of bookworms are completely governed by their passion for books. They haunt bookstores, prefer reading to viewing television, wander happily through libraries for hours, join book clubs, avidly read book reviews, and spend as many waking minutes as they can with books.

Bookworms are a special breed. They are easy to identify. You'll find them with their noses buried in books on buses and planes. You'll see them reading as they eat a solitary lunch in a cafeteria. You'll discover them perched under umbrellas on the beach and sitting on park benches concentrating on books. Wherever there are books, there will be bookworms close by.

Young children who are bookworms read under the covers with flashlights. Teenage aficionados of books rush through their homework to read. Older bookworms carry more library cards than credit cards.

Wherever bookworms live, their habitat is filled with books. There are books on coffee tables, countertops, window ledges, nightstands, and even stacked on the floor. Throughout a bookworm's home, favorites are resting in prominent places so they can easily be picked up and read. You could even mistake some bookworms' homes for a small branch library.

A bookworm's passion for the printed word never cools even though he or she has read hundreds of books and handled thousands more. They are entranced by great literature, capti-

1

vated by mysteries, enthralled by biographies, fascinated by histories, attracted to nonfiction, and drawn to all books, from encyclopedias to bestsellers.

The longer bookworms live with books, the more time they would like to spend with books. The cherished dream of most bookworms is to find a job that will let them be paid to read—a perfect combination of avocation with vocation.

A Bookworm's Dream— Reading from 9 to 5

Almost every job from insurance claims adjuster to architect to farmer requires some reading. But bookworms want something more—jobs that allow them to read for hours, not just a few brief minutes here and there. If they search the want ads carefully, they will find appealing jobs like these:

ACQUISITIONS EDITOR   Outstanding opportunity to work for children's book publisher. Responsibilities include selecting future publications, discovering new authors, and editing new titles.

ABSTRACTOR   Secondary information publisher seeks individual to write abstracts of journal articles on arts and literature. Must have strong writing and computer skills.

RESEARCHER   Information brokering firm needs researcher with science background to do on-line searching to gather information for biotech companies.

LIBRARIAN   Suburban library seeks reference librarian to answer phone queries and work at reference desk.

STORY ANALYST   Major movie studio requires experienced union story analyst to read scripts and write coverages.

This book is designed to help bookworms and other literary types discover jobs that will enable them to be paid for reading. Here is a bird's-eye view of some of the jobs you will read about in this book.

Library Careers

Libraries give bookworms the opportunity to have direct physical contact with their most valued possessions—books. What's more, no one who works in a library can adequately serve library patrons without doing some reading on the job. Upon investigation bookworms will discover that jobs in a library offer far more challenges than checking books in and out. And they will learn that more and more librarians are finding exciting careers in nonstandard library settings.

Book Publishing Careers

The most exciting aspect of a career in the book publishing industry is the opportunity to be part of creating a book. And there are jobs for bookworms at each step in the creation process. A manuscript must be acquired, edited, copyedited, set in type, and proofread. Then the finished product must be advertised and finally sold to a reader. The easiest way to discover the vast number of jobs that are available in publishing is to get your foot in the door by taking any kind of entry-level position.

Magazine and Newspaper Careers

Bookworms do not just burrow their noses in books. They read anything that is printed, especially magazines and newspapers. Although many of the editorial jobs in magazines and newspapers are similar to those in book publishing, there are many additional jobs. Think about all the letters that magazines and newspapers receive; someone has to read them and handle them appropriately. Then there are crossword puzzles to be created and wire service offerings and syndicated columns to be chosen. Within this variety of jobs, several offer bookworms the special opportunity to do nothing but read.

Glamourous Careers

Just because a person loves to read is no reason to think that person would only want to work in a quiet atmosphere surrounded by books. There are glamourous jobs that let bookworms combine reading with a chance to hobnob with movie stars or even work closely with them. After all, someone has to be hired to screen scripts to discover the right properties for a star and to handle a superstar's mail. And it's not just the movie industry, but also television and radio that offer bookworms jobs with a touch of glamour.

Education Careers

You can't hold many jobs in the education world without doing considerable reading to increase your knowledge. Classroom teachers have to read textbooks and accompanying teachers' manuals, professional journals, books, and magazines to enrich the curriculum for their students. University professors have to read and research to get their doctorates. Then they have to keep reading and researching to publish scholarly works that will help them get tenure. Reading jobs in education are not confined to teaching; for example, someone has to read all the applications students make to colleges.

Research Careers

It's fair to say that researchers are readers. Imagine yourself searching the library stacks to find books that trace the level of fashion consciousness of the wives of Henry VIII. Or possibly you could spend days on the computer exploring databases for information on the nutritional values of spinach. Such jobs may seem improbable, but they actually exist in the research job market. Jobs in research were once found primarily at universities. While most research remains university-centered, there are also research jobs with the government, businesses, and think tanks. Or you could choose a career as a historian, curator, or archivist and spend considerable time doing research.

Public Sector Careers

Because the government is the single largest employer in the United States, bookworms are likely to find many jobs that appeal to them in the public sector. At the federal level, senators and representatives need large numbers of people on their staffs to devote the majority of their time on the job to reading and answering constituent requests. Legislative analysts on the state level work for house and senate research departments. There is a need on the local level for people to search for property titles.

Private Sector Careers

With the explosion of information, almost every profession from engineering to medicine requires more reading by professionals. All large companies are looking for people to manage information and to retrieve needed information. One of the fastest growing businesses today is information services. Because the private sector is the area where the greatest number of jobs are, this is where bookworms will find the most jobs that let them be paid to read. From Wall Street to telecommuting on a hilltop, there are appealing jobs in the private sector for readers, like you.

More Careers for Bookworms

Bookworms tend to look for jobs that involve reading at places where books are traditionally found: libraries, schools, and publishing companies. While it is true that many jobs for readers are found in these places, there are less-well-known jobs that still involve reading. However, it does take some investigation to discover these jobs. Bookworms may be perfect for jobs as translators, storytellers, genealogy researchers, and news clippers for individuals and companies. Then, of course, there is the almost perfect job for a true bookworm being an author and writing a book.

Job Qualifications

Bookworms speak frequently and eloquently about their love for books. They consider books not only as prized possessions but also as true friends. However, a love of books and reading is not sufficient qualification for many jobs that require a significant amount of reading. Education really counts. In many cases, having a bachelor's degree isn't even enough. Quite often a master's degree is a prerequisite for being considered for a position. And there are many jobs for bookworms where holding double master's degrees or a doctorate would be helpful in getting the job. Fortunately, bookworms tend to want to study and receive as much education as possible. In preparing for a career, bookworms also need to realize that most jobs now require computer skills.

For Further Reading

John Adams demonstrated how well he knew what it was like to be a bookworm when he stated, "I read my eyes out and can't read half enough. . . . The more one reads the more one sees we have to read." Bookworms should become familiar with career books like these:

Carter, Carol and Gary June. *Graduating into the Nineties: Getting the Most Out of Your First Job after College.* New York, N.Y.: The Noonday Press, 1993.

Hirsch, Arlene S. *Careers Checklists.* Lincolnwood, Ill.: NTC Publishing Group, 1991.

Hopke, William E., ed. *The Encyclopedia of Careers and Vocational Guidance.* Chicago, Ill.: J. G. Ferguson Publishing Company, 1993.

Kennedy, Joyce Lain and Thomas J. Morrow. *Electronic Job Search Revolution.* New York, N.Y.: John Wiley & Sons, Inc., 1994.

Krantz, Les. *The Jobs Rated Almanac.* New York, N.Y.: World Almanac, 1992.

Le Compte, Michelle, ed. *Job Hunter's Sourcebook.* Detroit, Mich.: Gale Research Inc., 1993.

Occupational Outlook Handbook. Lincolnwood, Ill.: NTC Publishing Group, 1994.

VGM's Career Encyclopedia. Lincolnwood, Ill.: NTC Publishing Group, 1992.

Woodruff, Cheryl and Greg Ptacek. *150 Best Jobs for Liberal Arts Graduates* New York, N.Y. : John Wiley & Sons, Inc., 1992.

CHAPTER TWO

Library Careers
Making Information Available

L ibraries are the heart of our country's information system, and it is librarians who make this information available to more than 100 million people each year. As a librarian, you could be helping a teenager research a term paper, be cataloging books in a small office, or be overseeing the management of a university library. Whatever type of library work you are doing, the one constant is that you will always be surrounded by books. There is no more perfect place for a bookworm to find a job than in a library. If you are lucky enough to be working at the Library of Congress, there will be more than 22 million books in your workplace. You will even be able to find this book there because the Library of Congress tries to obtain copies of everything that is published in the United States.

Today, there are more than 119,000 libraries of all kinds in the United States. The work opportunities are almost endless. These libraries employ more than 168,000 librarians and other professionals. There are also jobs for support staff.

If you decide to work in a library, you will be in good company. Aristotle is probably the first well-known librarian. He put together a collection of books for his school in Athens, founded in 347 B.C. Before that there were libraries of papyrus scrolls and clay tablets, so there were librarians as long ago as 2000 B.C. In the British Museum, you can actually see an ancient library of clay tablets that was organized by an Assyrian king in about 700 B.C.

Two famous colonial statesmen, Benjamin Franklin and Thomas Jefferson, were also librarians. Pinch-penny Franklin started a subscription library, limiting its circulation to subscribers who paid a yearly fee. Not only did Jefferson catalog and classify materials for the University of Virginia library, he had his own personal library of 10,000 books. After the first Library of Congress burned, Jefferson's collection became the nucleus of the Library of Congress.

Familiar figures in this century who were librarians include J. Edgar Hoover, who worked at the Library of Congress while completing his law degree, and Mao Tse-tung, who was a library assistant at the Beijing University library. Mao carried periodicals to readers' tables and earned the same salary as a coolie.

Books are a librarian's major business. From 4,000 years ago until today, the focus of the librarian's job is much the same. Librarians collect, organize, and make information available to people.

Taking a Good Look at the Workplace

When you choose to work as a librarian, it may not always be in a modern, comfortable, spacious environment. You may be driving around all day in a bookmobile, working next door to a laboratory with all its varied odors, or handing out books at a remote Army base. There is a remarkable assortment of libraries in the United States, usually divided into these four categories: public, school, academic, and special.

But no matter whether a library is located at a zoo, in a law office, in a metropolitan area, or a small rural community, the librarian is the person who provides the essential services.

The Familiar Public Library

Bookworms are always familiar with the public libraries in their area. And there is no shortage of libraries for them to visit. The United States has more than 15,000 public libraries. These libraries, which are usually supported locally, vary greatly in size. You can get lost in the huge New York Public Library with its ten million books or find yourself in a small one-room library within the Arctic Circle in Alaska. However, no matter where a library is or how large or small it is, a librarian is needed to serve its users.

Regardless of their size, all public libraries have the same mission of serving the people who use them. This means having at least a core of reference books for everyone in the community, plus sections for children and adults. In some areas, libraries have special sections to meet the needs of that community. For example, the Detroit Public Library has a variety of materials on the history of the automobile.

Public libraries are no longer limited to traditional library buildings. In addition to roving bookmobiles, there are often services to retirement and nursing homes, jails, and hospitals.

School Libraries

The little old red schoolhouse did not have a library. Think back. Did your first school have a library or were there just books in the classroom? In recent years, more and more schools have put in libraries because teachers are asking their students to get information beyond what is in textbooks. Today, there are 92,628 school libraries.

The contents of school libraries tie closely to what is being taught at the schools. Obviously, high school libraries have a far wider range of material than those in elementary, middle, or junior high schools. Because today's school libraries are also storehouses for films, filmstrips, recordings, and graphic materials, they are now usually called library media centers or just media centers.

Academic Libraries

"Where are you going?" one college student asks another. Not surprisingly, the answer often is "the library." Students go to the library to find information, to research, and to study at the large tables or special study carrels.

Not all academic libraries are the same. Community college libraries tend to cater to the needs of adult learners. College libraries will vary greatly in size and scope. However, because of library networks and interlibrary loans, students can obtain just about any book that they want. University libraries are usually the largest academic libraries. Many have very specialized collections on specific subjects. The gigantic University of California library system has collections devoted to subjects like citrus fruits, California history, and oceanography. At a large university, you may find many separate libraries devoted to specific subjects located all over the campus.

Because of the knowledge boom that began in the 1950s and continues today, there has been a real increase in library building to store all this information. There has also been a fantastic increase in the use of computers to find where all this information is stored.

Special Libraries

"Special" is the key word to use in describing special libraries. These libraries deal with specialized subjects like pharmacology, law, transportation, and medicine. They have users who want special information, like the federal requirements to be followed in removing asbestos or the best treatment for Parkinson's disease. Without these special libraries, people would find it impossible to keep up with the latest information in so many areas—especially in scientific fields. What follows is just a glimpse at some of the special libraries that exist, and all these libraries have jobs for librarians.

Government Libraries

The Library of Congress, the National Library of Medicine, and the Library of Agriculture are three government libraries that have developed such extensive collections that they are considered national libraries. Besides these three libraries, the government operates an amazing number of libraries.

Each branch of the Armed Services has technical, educational, and recreational libraries on a nationwide and worldwide basis. The Navy even operates libraries on board ships. You will find libraries at Veterans Administration hospitals, the National Weather Service, the Patent and Trademark office, the Environmental Protection Agency, and in every department of the government. In addition, there are state libraries. The list of government libraries is almost endless.

Business Libraries

When employees at a firm need special information, they can often find it in the company library. Special libraries can be found in businesses like the following ones:

banks

accounting firms

steel companies

public utilities

television stations

aeronautics firms

investment houses

newspapers

food processing firms

advertising agencies

research institutes

telephone companies

Science Libraries

The vast amount of scientific knowledge that is constantly being discovered, updated, and changed in scientific fields like nutrition, marine biology, botany, physiology, biochemistry, zoology, and the health sciences necessitates libraries in such places as the following:

chemical companies

cosmetic companies

medical schools

health centers

hospitals

petroleum refineries

mining firms

medical societies

space-oriented companies

pharmaceutical firms

Would You Really Like To Be a Librarian?

You won't become a millionaire as a librarian, but you may have the opportunity to do quite a bit of reading. Being a bookworm, this should please you. However, you should realize that relatively few librarians have the luxury of sitting down on the job and reading a book from cover to cover. Of course, there are exceptions like the bibliographer at the National Library of Congress who has spent 40 years reading as he works on a bibliography of snow, ice, and permafrost.

The librarian sitting behind a desk at your local library is doing far more than reading; he or she spends a lot of time answering questions and helping patrons. But the librarian also has the chance to see new books coming into the library, to read reviews of books in an assigned area in order to find books to order, and to put together book lists. Some time may also be spent in scanning newspapers to update sources or to clip materials for various files.

Do You Have the Necessary Personal Qualifications?

Most library jobs require considerable versatility. However, there are certain qualities that most librarians share. Answer the following questions with a "yes" or a "no" to see if you possess most of these qualities.

		YES	NO
1.	Do you have a genuine love of books?	___	___
2.	Do you have a wide knowledge of books?	___	___
3.	Do you have the patience to keep searching until required materials are found?	___	___
4.	Do you have above-average academic ability?	___	___
5.	Do you have a good memory?	___	___
6.	Do you possess intellectual curiosity?	___	___
7.	Do you have the ability to make decisions?	___	___
8.	Do you have the ability to attend carefully to details?	___	___
9.	Do you like to work with computers?	___	___
10.	Do you have good oral and written communication skills?	___	___
11.	Do you have the ability to adjust to new procedures?	___	___
12.	Do you possess the knack of being tactful and courteous?	___	___
13.	Do you have a desire for continuing education?	___	___
14.	Do you have a genuine interest in helping people use libraries?	___	___
15.	Do you have the ability to get along with all types of people?	___	___

Thinking about Your Qualifications

Even if you answered "yes" to all of the above questions, it does not mean that you will be happy or successful in every library position. The personal qualities that would make you an excellent indexer might not make you an excellent children's librarian. In addition to the necessary personal qualifications, prospective librarians need to realize that there are considerable educational requirements for the position of professional librarian.

The Education of a Librarian

The amount of education needed to work in a library depends upon the job that you want to hold. If you want to be a professional librarian, you are going to have to obtain a master's degree in library science (M.L.S.). This will take you at least a year; however, a two-year program is becoming common. You will take basic courses in librarianship as well as advanced courses in such things as indexing, abstracting, cataloging, classification, administration, and automation.

Although a number of colleges offer the M.L.S. degree, you will probably want to attend one that has a program accredited by the American Library Association. Admission to these programs isn't easy. Not only will you need good college grades and an acceptable score on the Graduate Record Examination, you may also find knowledge of a foreign language helpful. Librarians are quite an educated group. After obtaining an M.L.S., many take courses in continuing education throughout their careers. And librarians with specific goals often go on to get certificates for advanced study programs, master's degrees in different fields, or even doctorates in library science.

Schooling Required for a Professional Librarian

PUBLIC LIBRARIES   If you want a really high administrative post in a very large library, having a master's degree in library science may not be enough. You may find it helpful to have a Ph.D. in library science or an advanced business degree.

SCHOOL LIBRARIES   If you like working with school-age children and are seriously considering being a school librarian, check the department of education's certification requirements in the state where you want to work. It may be sufficient to have a bachelor's degree in education plus courses in library science. More than likely, you will need to have a master's in educational media or library science.

ACADEMIC LIBRARIES   Librarians wishing to teach or hold top administrative posts will find it very helpful to have doctorate degrees.

SPECIAL LIBRARIES   Not only is a special librarian going to need an M.L.S., at least a bachelor's degree or possibly another master's degree is often required in the special field.

Schooling Required for Library Support Staff

Depending on where they work, the support staff of libraries have such titles as library technicians, library technical assistants, and library paraprofessionals. These library employees certainly don't need the years of education beyond high school that professional librarians do. In fact, it is even possible to get a support staff position with just a high school diploma and on-the-job training. Many libraries, nevertheless, prefer support staff to have completed a two-year college program in library technology. Some even require a bachelor's degree.

Librarians Talk about Their Work

Librarians love to read and feel that they need to read all the time because so much new material is constantly being published. However, most librarians can't read as much as they want because they have so many other things to do on their jobs. Librarians do manage to keep current with literature in their specific areas by relying on professional journals, book lists, and reviews.

The types of jobs librarians do are largely the same whether they are working in a public, school, academic, or special library. To give you a better picture of what librarians do, some librarians describe their work on the following pages.

Coordinator of Children's Services

A portable cart with at least 200 children's books sits by the desk of Chris Cairo, who is the coordinator of children's services at a major metropolitan library. Chris is a librarian who does a lot of reading, and she feels that most children's librarians also do considerable reading. The books on the cart are the ones the selectors at the main library and branch libraries wish to add to the library's collection. Chris will read the staff librarians' reviews on each of the books but only read 50 percent of the books from cover to cover. She reads the books to familiarize herself with the authors, illustrators, themes, and trends as well as to see which books the children's librarians in the library system want. She is responsible for ordering all the books for the metropolitan library system.

As coordinator of children's services, Chris also sets up various reading programs, supervises the creation of book lists on such subjects as "Reading Out Loud," "Indians of North America," and "Toddler Tales." Another responsibility is supervising all the children's librarians in the system. Chris, who has always loved to read, even takes books home in the evening to read to her children.

Senior Reference Librarian at a Magazine

Ronald Wilson confessed that he has always loved libraries. Even as a child, this avid reader spent considerable time in libraries. As senior reference librarian at *Newsweek*, he now gets paid to work in a library and read—a perfect situation for him. And he works with 6 librarians and 14 other staff members who really read on the job.

The librarians spend their days researching information for the magazine's writers, researchers, and correspondents, who must keep abreast of what is happening in the world. Each of these librarians is assigned a subject area or areas corresponding to the departments in the magazine. The librarian assigned to national affairs, for example, reads White House releases, the *National Journal*, and *Congressional Quarterly* magazines, as well as a variety of daily newspapers to keep files in this area up-to-date.

Ronald says you simply can't work on a news magazine without reading and keeping up with everything. In one day, he may answer questions about such diverse topics as Batman, Oprah Winfrey, and investment counselors. What kind of a background do you have to have to get jobs like his? Ronald has a very impressive resume with master's degrees in both public administration and library science. The other reference librarians are college graduates with advanced degrees in library science; many, like Ronald, have master's degrees in a variety of other specializations as well. How do you get these jobs? Most of the staff sent unsolicited resumes to the magazine. Ronald happened to meet the head librarian and learned of an opening for a librarian.

Ronald's natural habitat is libraries. Not only does he work full-time at *Newsweek*, he also works part-time doing reference work at a business research library. His job is quite different there because he spends his time helping students do research.

Library Assistant in a Newspaper Library

"The job is reading!" according to Dawn Hall, who handles several jobs in the library of a large newspaper. "It's very concise, exact, and fast reading," she says. As an indexer, she is assigned several pages of the newspaper to read carefully. She selects the stories the newspaper will want to keep on file in the electronic library system. Then subject headings are put on each story in red ink to indicate what the subject tags are.

As a processor, Dawn will read a newspaper story that has been indexed to get an idea of what it is about. Then she finds the story in the electronic library system and puts a header on it with such information as the date, writer, section and page in the newspaper, and the category. Headers must be placed on stories so they can be found again in the newspaper's electronic library system. Next, Dawn checks that the computer and newspaper versions of a story are the same.

Dawn will spend from 1½ to 4 hours a day indexing and processing stories. The rest of her time is spent doing research to answer questions for reporters and updating the vertical file on outside information the reporters may want. Because the newspaper library is open from 6:00 A.M. to midnight, Dawn and the other staff members work shifts.

Dawn's background includes a degree in education and an M.L.S. However, some of her coworkers have B.A.s in liberal arts, and some are just working on their college degrees. Dawn worked at a small newspaper after college before she found this job through a want ad in the newspaper.

Reference Librarian in the Social Sciences Division

People think that librarians sit around reading for their pleasure, but this is a myth, according to Kathy Barnard who works as a reference librarian in the social sciences division of a large public library. When you see her sitting at the desk, which is approximately 60 percent of her workday, much of her time is taken up in helping library patrons.

When she is not doing this, she is constantly scanning newspapers and general news magazines to update her assigned areas. For example, if she reads that a world leader has died, she will update the information in such references as *Statesman's Yearbook* or *Current Biography*. Kathy's job also requires her to read book reviews and to select new materials for an assigned area. When she is not at the desk, she is helping patrons find information by using indexes (both print and computer) and the library's on-line catalog, among other sources.

Reference Librarian in a Suburban Library

While working on her M.L.S. degree, Rhonda Hunnicutt is working in the reference section of a suburban library. She started at this library in a part-time job in the children's section. Previously, she worked as a schoolteacher. Like most reference librarians, some of her time on the job is spent reading reviews so that she can select new materials for an assigned area. Rhonda also reads articles in the vertical files to see which ones are out of date and should be discarded. She also has the responsibilities of keeping the college catalogs in order, working on the music section of the vertical file, and checking that the phone books are cataloged. Ninety percent of Rhonda's time is spent behind the desk helping patrons.

Director of Library at a Think Tank

Deborah Jones performs library services and acts as a "junior researcher." She works as an information and resource person for the staff of a think tank—one of those places where experts sit around and think. Then they write papers or speak on different topics. But it is Deborah and her staff who find so many of the sources that the experts read, whether it is about health care, education, foreign policy, or some other fascinating subject.

Deborah's job requires thoughtful reading. Each day she reads at least two newspapers trying to find articles that are related to research being done at the think tank. She also looks at news magazines and journals that are related to current research. Most of her time is spent trying to find information on topics currently being researched by the think tank staff.

Deborah's job requires creative research skills because she is always looking for hard-to-find information. Not only does Deborah have an M.L.S., she has taken many continuing courses in library science and some in computer science. For her job, she feels that a knowledge of computers is absolutely essential. Deborah obtained what she considers an extremely interesting job in an unusual way for this type of position—she answered a newspaper want ad. In her previous job, she was head of the reference department at a university library.

Reference Librarian in a Law Library

Steve Ries worked as an assistant in a law firm, went on to get his M.L.S., and went back to the same law firm as a librarian. Today, he has three assistants and a part-time employee. These people do such things as shelving books, filing new material, and keeping track of circulation. A college education is not required for these positions, but these employees do need to know how a library operates.

Steve's staff does not do as much reading as Steve does. He spends most of his time using books and the computer to search for the case studies that the lawyers in the firm need. For 75 percent of the workday, Steve can be found using the computer to find information.

Positive and Negative Aspects of Being a Librarian

Just like any other career, being a librarian has both positive and negative aspects. While this career may not let bookworms read as much as they like, it does allow them to spend time near their fondest possessions—books.

Good Things about Being a Librarian

1. Part of the time in your job you will be paid for doing what you love most—reading.

2. You will be working with people who share your love of books.

3. You will have the opportunity to share your knowledge of books with the library patrons.

4. You will be joining a profession that demands you keep learning about what is happening in the world.

5. You will have a job that lets you use all your creativity and initiative in searching for hard-to-find materials.

6. You can choose to be either a generalist or a specialist concentrating on a particular field of interest.

7. You can choose between working with people or working for the most part by yourself.

8. You can feel the reward of furthering other people's knowledge, whether they are esoteric researchers or third graders doing their first report.

Things to Consider before Becoming a Librarian

1. Considerable preparation is required for this career. Librarians usually need to have a master's degree.

2. Librarian's pay is not equal to other professions that require the same amount of schooling; however, salaries are going up for administrative positions.

3. You may have to cope at times with unreasonable demands and discourteous behavior from library patrons.

4. You will have to be able to stoop, lift, and stretch as you shelve or reach for books.

5. You will have to be willing to use computers in searching for information at most libraries.

6. You will not always work the typical 9-to-5 day. Libraries are open in the evenings and on weekends.

Getting a Job as a Librarian

If you just want a clerical or a technical job in a library, you can usually find this type of work by contacting a local library or looking at want ads in the newspaper. To get a job as a professional librarian, you will probably use other techniques, although some librarians have obtained jobs in those ways.

PART-TIME JOBS   You can begin paving the way for your first full-time job before you ever finish your education by working part-time in a library. Prior experience is always an added bonus on a résumé. Furthermore, getting your foot in the door with a part-time job can lead to a full-time job after graduation.

INTERNSHIPS AND WORK-STUDY PROGRAMS   You should also look into other options for experience like internships and work-study programs. Besides extremely sought-after internships at the Library of Congress and the National Library of Medicine, many research, academic, and special libraries have internships, which can lead to future jobs.

HELP ON CAMPUS   College placement services can really be helpful in finding a job. They have job listings, and many help with the writing of résumés and send your credentials to prospective employers. Don't overlook studying college bulletin boards and talking to faculty members, fellow students, and alumni when searching for a job.

HOTLINES   The phone is your friend when seeking a job. There are a fantastic number of hotlines that have the latest job listings. The American Library Assoiation can give you the numbers of state, regional, and association hotlines. Or look in the classified section of *American Libraries*.

WANT ADS   Most library journals have classified ad sections that list jobs. You can even advertise your own availability in some of these journals.

CONVENTIONS   Go to the annual conventions of library associations. Many have job placement programs. You can even send your credentials in before some conventions start.

DIRECTORIES AND BROCHURES   The *American Library Directory* lists all kinds of libraries in a two-volume directory. Its only weakness is that some school and special libraries don't return their forms so they aren't listed.

Another great resource with all kinds of hotline numbers and addresses is the *Guide to Employment Sources in the Library and Information Professions*. You can obtain single copies of this guide by writing to:

Office for Library Personnel Resources
American Library Association
50 East Huron Street
Chicago, IL 60611

FEDERAL GOVERNMENT LIBRARY JOBS   Don't overlook getting a job with the government. To work in many of the federal libraries you will have to establish civil service eligibility and be placed on the Office of Personnel Management (OPM) register in the geographic area in which you wish to be considered. Other agencies like the FBI, CIA, and Library of Congress have their own special procedures for getting a job, and applicants should make personal contact directly with the agencies.

Making a Living as a Librarian

There is good news about the amount of money librarians are earning. In 1994, an ALA survey showed that librarians' salaries increased slightly more than those in comparable occupations. The table below shows the mean salaries paid for particular positions in 1993 and 1994.

The ALA survey also showed that in 1994 beginning librarians with master's degrees in library science without any professional experience had mean earnings of $26,511. The range of salaries went from a low of $18,996 to a high of $48,800. Beginning salaries were highest in the North Atlantic States and lowest in the Southeast. You can get a better idea of what you might make as a librarian by studying the salaries listed in ads for librarians in professional journals.

Title	1994 Salary	1993 Salary
Director	$55,672	$53,331
Deputy/Associate/Assistant Director	$48,659	$47,070
Department Head/Branch Head	$40,544	$39,352
Reference/Information Librarian	$34,233	$33,001
Cataloger and/or Classifier	$33,928	$32,582
Children's and/or Young Adult Services Librarian	$33,588	$32,530

Source: Reprinted with permission of the American Library Association, excerpts taken from "ALA Survey of Librarian Salaries, 1994" by Mary Jo Lynch, Margaret Myers, and Jeniece Guy. Copyright © 1994 by ALA.

What Else Can You Do with a Library Degree?

Just because you graduated from college with a librarian's degree is no reason you have to become a librarian. Librarians can use their knowledge of books and library automation systems and excellent research and organizational skills in many other satisfying careers. Look at this list of book-related and information-related careers many librarians are following:

researcher

bookseller

archivist

editor

information consultant

indexer

storyteller

author

abstractor

information broker

records manager

database specialist

systems analyst

book reviewer

historian

information systems manager

Future Outlook for Librarians

There is definitely an explosion of printed material today. In just one day, according to Herbert S. White, former dean of the School of Library and Information Science at Indiana University, enough articles are written about chemistry to make up seven sets of the *Encyclopaedia Britannica*. This is sets, not volumes. And it is not just in the area of chemistry that volumes of material are being published; it's in every field that you can think of.

With all this information being published each day and because of their unique skills, librarians will play a major role in how it is handled. They will spend more time helping library patrons access needed materials. They will also find an increasing need for their skills in nonlibrary settings to analyze, evaluate, and organizae information.

For Further Reading

The image of a librarian sitting behind a desk checking books in and out is decidedly not a description of today's librarians. They have become information specialists who use computer technology to search for books in libraries throughout the world. Learn more about career opportunities for librarians by reading the following career books:

American Library Directory. New Providence, N.J.: Bowker, 1994.

Dewey, Barbara. Library Jobs: How to Fill Them, How to Find Them. Phoenix, Ariz.: Oryx, 1987.

Heim, Kathleen and Margaret Myers. Opportunities in Library and Information Science. Lincolnwood, Ill. : NTC Publishing Group, 1992.

Mount, Ellis, ed. Opening New Doors: Alternative Careers for Librarians. Washington, D.C.: Special Libraries Association, 1993.

Warner, Alice Sizer. Mind Your Own Business: A Guide for the Information Entrepreneur. New York, N.Y.: Neal-Schuman, 1987.

CHAPTER THREE

Book Publishing Careers
Connecting People with Books

Once upon a time authors did it all. They needed no one else to put out a book. An author wrote a book by picking up a stylus to etch the book onto clay tablets. Then the author shared the book with interested readers. No longer do books come directly from the author to you; things have changed. Authors still write books, but hordes of editors, proofreaders, designers, and printers work on books before they ever reach readers' hands. Should you decide to work in the book publishing industry, you could be one of these people.

In the United States there are more than 2,000 book publishers. Together, they publish approximately 50,000 hardcover and paperback books every year and employ more than 75,000 people. A career in this industry can be just right for a confirmed bookworm because so many jobs in book publishing involve considerable reading.

Did you realize that there are jobs that would let you:

- read manuscripts all day and decide whether they will be published,
- change an author's presentation to make it more powerful,
- sell books to bookstores and schools,
- find typographical errors that a printer has made, and
- even write your opinion of books?

A Glimpse into the Book Publishing Industry

Browse through a bookstore, and you will find children's books, travel books, religious books, handyman books, cookbooks, romances, and an amazing number of other kinds of books. Most of these books are called trade books, and they make up about one-third of all the books sold. Believe it or not, more textbooks for use by students from kindergarten through college are sold than trade books. There is also a market for reference books like dictionaries, encyclopedias, and atlases as well as for scholarly books put out by university presses. Some publishing companies will put out a wide variety of books, while others will only fill a particular niche.

Just as books come in all sizes so do publishing companies; however, most are small publishing houses. The largest companies may employ thousands of people, while the smallest may only have two employees—the publisher and an assistant. You are more likely to have a specific job like copyeditor or proofreader at a larger firm, while at a smaller firm you could wear several hats at once.

You may find it helpful to know what the usual organization chart looks like in a large publishing company.

Editor-in-Chief

Executive Editor

Editor—Managing or Acquisitions

Associate Editor

Assistant Editor

Editorial Assistant

Naturally, this chart will look slightly different at each publishing house. Assistant editor, instead of editorial assistant, is often the entry-level position. Copyeditors can be part of the above hierarchy as assistant or associate editors; however, in large houses they are usually found in a separate department.

Getting Your Feet Wet

Starting as an Editorial Assistant

You'll never get bored starting in the publishing industry as an editorial assistant because of the large variety of tasks that you will be required to do. There will be plenty of tedious jobs like typing, filing, verifying facts, retyping manuscripts, and returning unacceptable manuscripts. The good news is that you will probably be able to do quite a bit of reading on the job as soon as you know how the publishing house works.

Much of your reading will center on going through the "slush" pile, which is the accumulation of unsolicited manuscripts that drown most publishers. You will be evaluating the potential of each manuscript. It will be painful to read some of these efforts. On the other hand, you may be the one to discover a new Hemingway. You won't be able to select manuscripts for consideration just because you like them; they will have to fit in with what the publishing house prints. A Christian publishing house will not be looking for steamy romance stories.

Starting as a Clerk

Janet Peterson entered the publishing industry as a clerk, moved up to become a secretary, and is now editorial administrator/ permissions editor. Janet was definitely not a bookworm while she was in school. Today, however, she finds that she is reading at least one-third of the time on her job. Janet feels that reading is essential if you plan to grow in a job. She has to keep up with what is happening in the publishing industry.

As editorial administrator, Janet is resourceful in managing information and interacting with the education and publishing communities. In her role as permissions editor, she reviews requests and grants permission to teachers and authors to use information from products published by her publisher. Janet also negotiates with authors and publishers for permission to use their materials.

Starting at a Children's Publishing House

Sometimes getting an entry-level job can be based upon who you know. A burned-out schoolteacher found a job as a junior editor at a children's publishing house because she knew someone who worked there. Today, this former teacher is a children's book editor. As an editorial assistant, called "junior editor" at her company, her work was not glamorous. She typed, filed, researched, and learned to edit with the help of an editor. Gradually, she was given books to edit.

Climbing the Editorial Ladder

After one or two years as an editorial assistant, you will probably begin to move up the editorial ladder. The irony is that the higher you climb, the less time you will be able to devote to reading because so many administrative tasks intervene. Very senior editors find that their job-related reading has become their homework. They do it while they commute, in the evening, on weekends, and on holidays.

Assistant Editor—A Reader's Job

Up one notch from an editorial assistant, the assistant editor at most publishing houses will be doing primarily copyediting and proofreading. At this level, bookworms should be in heaven because there is so much reading to do. Be warned, though, some assistant editors will be weaned away from their reading to become involved with the editorial production of books. This can mean working with the art department or designers on page layout and illustrations.

Copyediting

Copyeditors usually get manuscripts from editors or assistant editors who have worked on the content and organization. They fix what is still wrong. No two copyeditors have exactly the same job. At some houses, they may do considerable rewriting, while at others they are only marking typographical errors. In either case, copyeditors are responsible for checking spelling, grammar, and punctuation. They look for inconsistencies in copy, such as first boarding a plane and later disembarking from a ship (rather than the plane). They also have to find and eliminate repetitions. They read an entire manuscript paragraph by paragraph, line by line, and finally word by word. Some copyeditors use computers, but many prefer to do their job by using good old-fashioned pencils directly on manuscripts.

A manuscript is always read more than once because copyediting also involves keeping track of the plot and making sure that events fall into the correct slots on a time line. Often the first reading is quick to get the overall idea of the manuscript. Then corrections are made. After a final rereading, the manuscript goes back to the author, who may make changes, which are also copyedited. The manuscript is checked again when it comes back from the typesetter and every time any changes are made in the copy.

Proofreading

Do you have the eyes of an eagle? Are you good at finding typographical errors on the printed page? Do you have the ability to scrutinize manuscripts closely? Are you a good speller? Even if you answer "yes" to the above questions, you will need to be able to prove your proofreading skills by taking a test that includes a spelling section before you will be hired.

Proofreading involves checking that copy from the printer exactly matches the manuscript. To proofreaders, finding inconsistencies is almost like a game. Training is required for this job. Many proofreaders have gone to schools; more have probably learned on the job. Although all copyeditors do some proofreading, much of it is done by free-lancers.

Assistant Editor—Romances

At Harlequin Books, which publishes 70 paperback romance books each month, the entry-level position on the editorial side is assistant editor. To obtain this position you have to demonstrate the ability to read a book and know if it meets the company's standards, fix a story so it flows, critique a plot, line edit, and write cover copy. Most successful applicants have degrees in English.

Assistant editors at Harlequin begin working under senior editors, who supervise their training. One thing they have to learn is how to write revision letters, which explain changes editors think would improve an author's manuscript. Assistant editors will read senior editors' revision letters as part of acquiring this skill. They will also read submissions from the "slush" pile to find possible acquisitions.

Each assistant editor is assigned a stable of authors who regularly write Harlequin books. He or she will edit these books and also begin to find his or her own repeat authors from the "slush" pile.

Associate Editor—A Varied Position

After working for a few years as an assistant editor, the next step at many companies is associate editor. It's a good promotion for a reader because it means less clerical work, and you will still be doing considerable reading. Of course, at the same time, your responsibilities are going to increase. This usually means more contact with authors, especially because you are going to have the authority to make more changes in manuscripts. You will be making rewrite suggestions for cuts and additions and will have far more leverage in how a book is edited. And you will also begin to become involved in the acquisition of new books.

An Associate Editor

Karen Zack Ingebretsen started working as a proofreader at Time-Life Books ten days after her graduation from college. She willingly skipped the ceremony in order to get a jump on the June crowd of job seekers by interviewing on her commencement day. Karen was required to take a typical proofreading test. After getting the job, Karen, who truly enjoys reading, found out that her job consisted entirely of reading. For forty hours a week, Karen read manuscripts for everything from recipe books to opera librettos in foreign languages that she couldn't speak. In two years, her job disappeared due to a layoff.

Karen then became a production/copyeditor at Prentice-Hall. As a production editor, she worked with the art department on concepts for illustrations and covers. She was also responsible for designing interiors, trafficking schedules, and monitoring the flow of manuscript and proof between the typesetter and author. This part of the job only took 25 percent of her time. She spent the rest of the time reading as she edited copy. Once again Karen lost her job to a layoff.

Karen began to believe that she would never last long enough on a job to get the seniority that was needed to survive a layoff. She considered many alternatives, including teaching English in a foreign country and joining the Peace Corps. However, before she could implement a career change, she acquired a new job at Editing, Design and Production as a project editor. This job still required Karen to read for 75 percent of her workday. The company took over the production of books for publishing houses that had small staffs. At this job, she was doing the same work as at her previous job, with the added dimension of keeping the publisher, who was now a client, informed of the progress on a book that she was working on. Subsequently, marriage brought a move to Chicago where Karen found a job as a senior editor at a general reference publisher. Karen has been promoted twice at the Chicago firm and is now an associate editor. She finds that she does less and less hands-on editing as she climbs the editorial ladder; rather, she is supervising the work of others, which is typical throughout the publishing industry. She still spends time reading, though not as much. A large portion of her time goes to planning projects and projecting and tracking project costs. She also spends a good deal of time in meetings. Karen continues to do both professional reading (*Publisher's Weekly, BP Report, School & Library Journal*) as well as reading about current events, which is essential when you work for a general reference publisher. As new books are planned, she becomes an "instant expert" on their subjects through extensive background reading.

Editor—Managing or Acquisitions

What an editor does varies greatly from company to company. Some publishing houses have both managing and acquisitions editors. At other houses, an editor will be both a managing and an acquisitions editor. How much editors read truly depends on what their responsibilities are. Some will still do quite a lot of reading at their offices, while others will spend most of their time working on the business side of publishing.

Managing Editor

These editors are in charge of day-to-day operations. They see that schedules are maintained and supervise junior editors. Managing editors typically oversee the work of the copyeditors, proofreaders, and in many cases, the designers and illustrators, who are responsible for the way books will look.

Acquisitions Editor

At times being an acquisitions editor can be quite a glamorous job. These are the editors who have long chats and lunches with famous authors, go to autograph parties, and attend book fairs all over the world. They have the task of bringing in and signing up new books and authors and working with literary agents. They are also supposed to come up with new book ideas.

Editor at a Trade Book Company

The editorial assistant who was described earlier worked her way up the ladder until today she is an editor of children's books. At the company where she works, she wears the hats of both a managing and an acquisitions editor.

Every fourth week she becomes an acquisitions editor and goes through as many as 75 books in a week. Not all of the 75 books are read cover to cover. However, after careful scanning and skimming, each book is thrown in a pile indicating its future. This editor clearly knows what she likes and what her company is looking for. She discusses her acquisition choices with other editors. If the majority approve a book, it is sent to the marketing department for a "yes" or "no" vote.

While wearing the hat of managing editor, this editor oversees the production of as many as 20 books in a year. Not only does she decide on text changes, she also acts as a copyeditor, which is something not all editors do.

In describing the pluses and minuses of her job, this editor points out that the job is not dull or routine. Because the subject matter varies greatly, the opportunity to learn something new is always there. The one negative to her job is the tension you feel when you fall behind on your schedule.

Executive Editor

A large publishing house may have an executive editor, who oversees the assistant and associate editors and handles many responsibilities typically given to the editor-in-chief. Executive editors often direct the overall planning and editorial content of the company's publications. They spend time coordinating art, text, pre-press, and manufacturing to ensure proper control over production scheduling, implementation of technology, quality, and cost. In addition, they may develop long-range plans and monitor developments in the publishing industry to assess the long-range implications of trends to their companies.

Executive Editor at World Book

For 30 years, Dale Jacobs has been at World Book, the publishers of *The World Book Encyclopedia*, *Childcraft*, and other reference materials for home and school. Dale's career has truly been a bookworm's delight. He describes his first job as an assistant editor at World Book as a reading job with lots of writing, too. Dale read books, periodicals, and leading newspapers to get information for revising encyclopedia articles and also read and revised contributors' articles. Although all of his jobs have involved considerable reading, Dale did the most reading when he was the social sciences editor and had to do wide reading to keep abreast of what was happening in this area. In his present position, he often spends half of his day reading memos, correspondence, original and edited manuscripts, and other revision proposals. He also spends a portion of his day doing background reading in the *Wall Street Journal*, *New York Times*, *Time*, *Newsweek*, and other materials related to the creative and business side of publishing. Dale says that bookworms will have a head start in finding a job with World Book because the company is looking for employees who have read widely to keep up-to-date with current events.

Editor-in-Chief

At the top of the editorial ladder is the editor-in-chief, who has almost always climbed the ladder rung by rung to reach this position. This job requires great involvement in the business side of publishing books. The editor-in-chief makes major decisions on budgeting, scheduling, acquisitions, and marketing strategies. Time is also spent on developing ideas for new books and monitoring the progress of projects. Only a very limited amount of time is spent reading and editing manuscripts.

Editorial Director at Globe Pequot Press

Mike Urban has been in the publishing industry for 17 years. To get his first job as an editorial assistant at a publisher of medical journals, he actually had to take a typing test. Although half of his time on this job was spent doing clerical work, the other half was devoted to learning editorial skills like copyediting, proofreading, and page layout. After a year, Mike moved to Rand McNally to work as a research assistant updating listings in travel guides. In this job, as well as in positions as assistant and associate editor, Mike did tons of reading and some writing of travel literature. A move to World Book to become a project editor and later a senior editor gave Mike experience in production tasks. This job also involved considerable reading and research. His next job, however, at NTC Publishing Group as acquisitions editor, gave Mike the perfect job for bookworms; he was reading all the time as he reviewed new and unsolicited manuscripts.

Today, Mike is editorial director at Globe Pequot, a medium-sized trade travel publisher. Now at the top of the editorial ladder, Mike is doing less reading and concentrating more on administrative tasks. He is in charge of the manufacture and production of 80 new and revised books each year. Plus, he is spearheading the company's participation in multimedia and electronic publishing. Mike says publishing books involves a lot of tedious work, but when he holds a new book in his hands and knows that he had a hand in its creation, it gives him a rewarding feeling.

Publisher or President

At many publishing houses, there is a publisher or president at the top directing the entire operation. This is not a hands-on manuscript job. It involves supervising every department of the company. This job has a lot of reading, but it is reading memos, financial statements, and professional journals.

Publisher at Free Spirit Publishing

Not all publishing companies are large. At Free Spirit the publisher is also president. In the early days, she was also business manager and office manager. Today, the company has a staff of 13 full-time employees, including a marketing manager, a business manager, and an office manager, plus employees doing various jobs from order processing and shipping to editorial assistance. Editors and graphic designers are all hired free-lance.

Not all publishers make their way through the editorial ranks to achieve their positions. Judy Galbraith was a teacher who started Free Spirit after purchasing the publishing rights to her first book, which had been published by another publisher. The company has grown steadily and has published 70 titles since its inception in 1983. Judy loves to read but is compelled to devote her office hours to the publishing business. However, at home, after work, and on weekends and airplanes, she spends hours reading trade publications and manuscripts. Publishers tend to be bookworms.

Indexing—Another Publishing Job for Bookworms

If you like the idea of doing free-lance work in the publishing industry, indexing is an excellent job possibility because few companies have full-time indexers on their staff. Furthermore, some publishing houses leave indexing up to authors, who in turn usually look for free-lance indexers to do this work.

In creating an index, an indexer makes an alphabetical list of a book's contents and lists page numbers where each item is discussed. Here is a job where a bookworm is being paid to read a book. Although books on every subject from podiatry to forestry are indexed, you will need some experience in a subject to index a book. Most indexers have advanced degrees and specialize in certain subjects. The job also requires organizational skills and the ability to determine what is important in a book. Plus, you almost have to be able to handle a computer because indexing has gone high tech. Doing indexes on 3 × 5 cards is a thing of the past for most indexers. In addition, indexers must be able to function well under pressure. Indexing is always a rush job because indexers are the last in line to get copy.

Acquiring Indexing Skills

You need some training to become an indexer. A publisher is going to expect you to know certain things. Unfortunately, there are few indexing classes. Some can be found at colleges that have schools of library science. The United States Department of Agriculture (USDA) offers two correspondence courses. For information about these courses, write to:

Graduate School, USDA
Correspondence Study Program
South Agriculture Bldg., Room 1114
14th & Independence, SW
Washington, DC 20250

The National Federation of Abstracting and Information Services (NFAIS) offers seminars in indexing that can help both beginning and experienced indexers. This organization also publishes the *Career Guide to Careers in Indexing and Abstracting*, which is available for a fee. Contact this organization at:

NFAIS
1518 Walnut Street, Suite 307
Philadelphia, PA 19102

The indexing field is a small one. Many indexers belong to The American Society of Indexers. Through membership in this organization, indexers get newsletters, other publications at a discount, a subscription to *The Indexer*, a discount on conference fees, plus the opportunity to talk with other indexers at local organizations of the society. Information about this organization can be obtained by writing to:

The American Society of Indexers
P.O. Box 386
Port Aransas, TX 78373

Working as an Indexer

You can make a living as a free-lance indexer. Although what you are paid will vary from area to area, an experienced indexer averages about $30 an hour. You will earn more if you are very fast or handle very complicated material. The most common method of billing is charging for each indexable page (typically, $2.50 to $5.00 per page). You get a job as an indexer through contacts with editors and other indexers and by sending résumés to publishing companies.

An Indexer at World Book

David Profelski feels very lucky to work at a company as an indexer. There are not many of these jobs. After college, he had no idea of what he would like to do except he felt publishing was an intriguing area. He found a job at Encyclopaedia Britannica as an indexer and has remained in this field throughout most of his career. He spent nine years at home working as a free-lancer doing his indexing on index cards before purchasing a computer. David has been at World Book since 1988.

Indexing has become far more mechanized in the past 15 years. Indexers no longer have to worry so much about clerical details and are freer to concentrate on the quality of what they are producing. The advent of the computer has also cut the number of indexers required on David's company's staff.

David enjoys his job because he likes to read and especially likes reading a variety of materials and learning so much about different areas. He approaches indexing as a craft and tries to do the best possible job on each index. However, the job has some negative aspects. He spends his entire day looking at a terminal, and there is considerable clerical work keying words in and checking for accuracy. He also works under tremendous pressure to get jobs done.

Literary Agents Get Books to Editors

Just because an author writes a book doesn't mean you'll ever be able to find it on a library shelf. It isn't easy for an author to get a book published, especially because many publishing companies won't even look at a manuscript unless it is submitted by a literary agent. In this country, there are more than 300 literary agencies. Whether an agency is run by one person or has hundreds of employees, the dream is to find the next bestseller.

Literary agents represent authors to publishers, and they also act as negotiators between the two. Today, due to time restraints, more publishers are relying on literary agents to produce new authors and materials.

Literary agents' days are never routine. They always buzz with activity. A typical day may include working with authors, editors, lawyers, and accountants. Agents may suggest changes to an author that will make a book marketable, mediate a conflict between an author and an editor, as well as boost the flagging spirits of yet another author. They may try to convince an editor that an author in their stable has just written a novel that will become an American classic or at least sell more than 10,000 copies. The agents may wheel and deal with lawyers to get the best contract for a first-time author. They may check recent sales figures with an accountant. More than likely they will also suffer rejection. Some books that they absolutely love will never be sold to a publisher. Others may take years to sell. Rejection, even frequent rejection, is an accepted part of a literary agent's job.

Between all the paperwork and the never-ending phone calls, literary agents do not have a lot of time for reading during office hours. Yet reading is an important part of a literary agent's work; it is the only way to discover books to sell to editors. So reading time must be snatched whenever possible at the office, but most of it will be done after hours.

You don't just set up shop as a literary agent. Most literary agents are former editors who have an eye for manuscripts that will sell. They can read the first 30 pages of a manuscript or the proposal for a book and know right away whether or not it has possibilities. Besides having the ability to recognize a saleable manuscript, a literary agent is really a jack-of-all-trades who has the ability to:

- handle people effectively,
- shape an author's career,
- know where different manuscripts can be sold,
- negotiate contracts, and
- help authors edit their work.

Bookworms will enjoy even an entry-level position as an assistant in a literary agency. The job involves many of the same duties as an editorial assistant. However, because many of the agencies are small, an assistant at an agency will be doing more reading than in a large publishing house. The job could include reading manuscripts and writing reviews along with typing and filing correspondence to authors and publishers, as well as scheduling meetings among authors, agents, and publishers. Some assistants become full-fledged agents or editors at publishing firms, while a few start their own agencies.

Book Reviewers Are Paid for Their Opinions

Imagine getting a free copy of a book and also getting paid to read it. That's what happens if you are a book reviewer. Because the job is so appealing, there are a great number of book reviewers. Unfortunately, only a few of them are able to make their living at this job. For that reason, book reviewing is usually done by free-lancers.

Book reviewers are normally paid for each review. How much you receive for a review depends on the size of the newspaper or magazine, the length and complexity of the review, and occasionally on your reputation as a reviewer. You could receive nothing except a new book or as much as $500. By selling the same review to different markets in geographically separated areas or in shorter or longer versions, it is possible to increase your income. You might be able to make as much as $1,000 for a single review.

To become a book reviewer you will need to be far more than an avid reader; you also have to have writing ability. You can learn how to be an expert book reviewer by studying book reviews that others have written and by taking courses. Just working in the publishing industry will also give you some of the experience you need.

Reading a book is the easiest part of being a book reviewer. The hardest is finding someone who wants you to write a review. Dave Wood, the book editor of the *Minneapolis Star Tribune*, has the names of 250 book reviewers in his file. During a typical year, less than half of these reviewers will actually write reviews for the newspaper. And only 50 to 60 will be used frequently to write reviews.

The road to being one of the lucky people chosen to write a review is a rough one. What you have to do is send a résumé and samples of your work to newspapers and magazines. This frequently accomplishes nothing more than getting your name in a Rolodex file. You can also send unsolicited reviews. If an editor is looking for the book you reviewed, you may be on your way to becoming paid for reviewing books.

Book reviewers with some experience, even if it is for a small newspaper or magazine, can join the National Book Critics Circle. Members' names, along with their specialties, are put into a directory that book editors use to find reviewers. The organization also has a newsletter as well as regional and national seminars that provide information that is helpful to book reviewers. You can join the National Book Critics Circle if you write a minimum of three book reviews a year and pay a fee. For information, contact:

Patricia Holt, Membership Vice President
National Book Critics Circle
582 30th Street
San Francisco, CA 94131

Reviewing Books for a Magazine

One of the first places in which books are reviewed is *Publishers Weekly*. Valiska Gregory reviews four to six children's books each month for this magazine. At times, the books are so new that she is reading from color proofs that are not even bound together.

When she reviews a children's book, Valiska tries to assess the author's purpose from the text and illustrations. She always reads a book more than once. She doesn't follow any particular format in writing her reviews, but she does try to give an indication of what the book is about as well as an assessment of the book's literary and artistic merit. She often compares a book to similar ones.

Valiska, who is an author and a poet as well as a free-lance book reviewer, obtained her job through personal contacts. While attending a publishing course, she met a woman who became an editor of the magazine that uses her reviews.

Reviewing Books for a Newspaper

Working in the library at a newspaper gave Betsy Caulfield the opportunity to meet the book editor and led to her becoming a free-lance book reviewer. Being a dedicated bookworm, Betsy always read book reviews. She got the idea of becoming a reviewer because she frequently disagreed with reviewers of books that she had read and wanted to share her opinion with others. She now reviews about one book each month after reading the entire book to get its essence.

Selecting Books for the Book Clubs

Every few weeks, millions of homes, especially the homes of bookworms, receive selection magazines from book clubs. Besides the well-known Book-of-the-Month Club and Literary Guild, there are specific clubs that cater to interests ranging from cooking, astronomy, and religion to photography, farming, and ecology. Children's books are offered through many of these clubs as well as separate children's clubs. Each club will typically offer the opportunity to purchase new selections along with backlist titles.

Like the climber who reaches the top of Mount Everest, a bookworm who becomes a selector for a book club has reached the summit of his or her dreams. This job involves reading books and then deciding which ones should be offered to members of the clubs. At some clubs, all the selectors are in-house editors reading literally from 9 to 5. At other houses, the editors do most of their reading at home while attending to marketing and administrative chores on the job. Most houses will also use some free-lance selectors, who do a first read of a manuscript and are typically paid between $50 and $100 (the highest) per manuscript.

Bookworms who become selectors usually have bachelor's degrees behind their names. Their degrees certainly don't have to be in English but usually are in some area of liberal arts. It is possible to get a job as a selector right after graduating from college. But many get this job after working as administrative assistants, copyeditors, or at some other job in publishing. Don't bother applying for this job unless you are a speed reader. You should be able to read a thousand pages in 12 to 15 hours.

Working as a Book Selector

"Sometimes, the pages just turned themselves," according to Jaye Isler, who was an editorial assistant at a major book club. At other times, she didn't even complete a book because it wasn't right for the book club's members. Jaye, like other selectors, is a confirmed booklover. She confesses that she would far rather meet an author than a Hollywood star.

Jaye's job as an editorial assistant was a busy one with long hours. She didn't usually read manuscripts at the office but was involved in such things there as making sure that books that were to be listed in the club's magazine were in stock, and that there were pictures of these books. She also checked that the copy describing the books was accurate. At any one time, she was working on book information that would go in any one of eight selection magazines. Also, she spent considerable time in meetings and negotiating with publishers to attain the rights to a book.

Outside of the office, Jaye read for approximately ten hours a week. During that time, she would read two or three books to determine if the club should offer them to its members. When selectors begin working at Jaye's book club, they learn how to do their job by reading book evaluations that experienced selectors have made. At first, their evaluations are checked to make sure they understand what the club is looking for. "The longer one selects books for a club," Jaye says, "the easier it becomes to tell which books will satisfy the club members." Today, Jaye is spending much of her time writing; however, she still spends some time reading and making selections for the book club.

Owning Your Own Bookstore

To a bookworm, owning a bookstore must seem like the best of all possible worlds. You can choose the books that you want for the store and look at new books before they are even bound. Before Shirley Mullin became a bookstore owner, she was a teacher. Now she owns two children's bookstores, called Kids Ink.

Bookstore owners get to do a lot of job-related reading. Shirley sees most new children's book from six to nine months before they are published. When she first sees a book, she is usually not looking at the finished copy but at galleys for the book. She reads all the children's picture books herself but doesn't have time to read all the other books, so she farms some of them out to her staff. Shirley often reads reviews, which usually come out after she has read the galleys for new books. By reading the reviews, she can see if she has missed seeing any promising new books or if she wishes to reexamine any books that she has read. Shirley is helped in her selection process by knowledgeable publishing company representatives and her own staff.

Working at a Bookstore

Along with libraries, bookstores seem the perfect habitat for bookworms. And there are 20,000 retail bookstores ranging from small specialized shops to superstores as possible workplaces. In a bookstore, surrounded by books, a bookworm may not have too much opportunity to read on the job. However, bookstore employees are encouraged to read book reviews and books so that they can help customers find the books they want. At many stores, the owners and managers also want employee input on what books should be added to a store's stock. An added dividend for bookstore employees can be purchasing books for a discounted price.

Part of the recent strong growth in sales of trade books is because of the emergence of book superstores. These stores will stock from 30,000 to 80,000 titles. And the managers of these stores are actively searching for bookworms who really know books—from popular bestsellers to less well-known offerings from small publishing houses.

More Jobs Associated with Books

The more you learn about all the steps involved in bringing a book from author to reader, the more you'll know about the great variety of jobs that will actually let you read books. Taking an entry-level job or an internship are two ways many bookworms have become acquainted with interesting jobs like the following ones:

Designing a Book

Someone has to decide just what a finished book is going to look like so it will appeal to readers. All the artwork, the headings, and the arrangement of the material on the pages have to be related to what is said on the pages. Each book needs to have a design theme. A job working in this area can tie your interest in books with an artistic background.

Illustrating a Book

Illustrations are an important part of many books and must tie closely to the text. In order to do this successfully, the illustrator needs to carefully read the manuscript. Children's books and textbooks are usually full of illustrations. At times, illustrating is done in-house, but more often it is done by free-lance illustrators.

Selling a Book

For a bookworm, it's a lot more enjoyable to sell books than to sell aluminum siding or automobiles. Working as a sales representative for a publisher not only gives you the chance to read many of the books that you are trying to sell, you also get to talk about them to bookstore owners, buyers for chains, and librarians. If you are selling textbooks, you will talk to both teachers and selection committees. No matter where you are selling books, your commission will be based on how well you know the product—books. Being a sales representative is a great career for a bookworm because the more you read, the more you earn, and you will also get the added benefit of traveling.

In this position everyone is a beginner. The better you sell, the better your territory will be. Success in sales can also lead to management job offers in the home office. Some sales representatives even branch off on their own and become independent representatives.

More Career Possibilities

Even more career opportunities exist for bookworms. Besides the many careers that have been mentioned, you may want to investigate some of the following career areas:

marketing

promotion

publicity

corporate staff

advertising

production

public relations

You won't just find jobs with publishers. Book jobbers and distributors, direct and subscription mail sales organizations, and book chains are other areas where bookworms can find jobs that let them be close to books in some way.

Earning Your Living in the Book Business

The book publishing industry is definitely not a get-rich-quick place to work. Entry-level employees are poorly paid. Editorial assistants average $21,000 a year. Editors average $44,000 a year, and editor-in-chiefs average $77,800, according to a 1994 survey in *Publishers Weekly*.

Furthermore, because most of the book publishing industry is centered in New York and Chicago, your climb up the ladder will involve paying a premium price for your living quarters. Remembering that your salary should increase a little with each rung of the ladder and the fact that you are working with books should help bookworms overcome the negatives involved in working in book publishing.

Preparing Yourself for a Career in Book Publishing

Working in book publishing may not be well-paid, but it is an exciting field that many college graduates want to enter. There is strong competition for entry-level jobs, especially at major publishing houses. You will need a college degree. You will also need to excel in your usage of the English language. It will be a definite plus if you can use a computer.

Getting experience by working with books in some capacity will make you a stronger candidate for a job. Working part-time in a bookstore or library can be helpful. Finding a part-time job with a publishing house is even better because you can then show actual work experience in the industry. Working as an intern at a publishing company will also strengthen your résumé. Both part-time jobs and internships can lead to job offers because they let publishing companies become acquainted with your work. You can find out what internships are available by looking at directories listing internships. You will find these directories in the reference section of the library.

Attending book publishing courses, conferences, workshops, and seminars will increase your insight into what the industry is like. Reading *Publishers Weekly* will let you know what is happening in publishing. It has a calendar that gives current information on courses, workshops, and seminars; there is even a jobs section in the magazine. It is also smart to become acquainted with Literary Market-Place (LMP). This directory has the names, addresses, and phone numbers of book publishers in the United States. The publishers are even classified by subject matter. You will also find information about book courses, conferences, and events. There are lists of literary agents, book clubs, and foreign publishers as well as information about acquisitions and mergers in the industry.

A Glimpse into the Future

The demand for books should grow in the next five years as the population increases in the book-buying age group, and more children are in school. Besides, the foreign market for books is growing. And as the demand for books increases, the need for employees, especially in editorial, marketing, and administrative positions, should increase. New opportunities for bookworms will emerge in the area of nonprint formats for books including audio books and CD-ROM disks.

For Further Reading

Isn't it ironic that one of the best ways to prepare for a career in book publishing is by reading to learn all you can about the industry? As Lord Chesterfield wrote in a letter to Lord Huntington, "The best companions are the best books." The following books should become your companions if you are serious about learning more about a career in book publishing.

Berner, R. Thomas. *The Process of Editing*. Needham Heights, Mass. : Allyn, 1990.

Carter, Robert A. *Opportunities in Book Publishing Careers*. Lincolnwood, Ill.: NTC Publishing Group, 1987.

Datus, C., Jr. *A Guide to Book Publishing*. Seattle, Wash.: University of Washington Press, 1989.

Dessauer, John P. *Book Publishing—The Basic Introduction*, New York, N.Y.: The Continuum Publishing Company, 1993.

Gross, Gerald, ed. *Editors on Editing: An Inside View of What Editors Really Do*. New York, N.Y.: Grove-Atlantic, 1993.

Herman, Jeff. *Insider's Guide to Book Editors, Publishers, and Literary Agents*. Rocklin, Calif.: Prima Publishing, 1993.

Literary MarketPlace—The Directory of American Book Publishing. New York, N.Y.: R.R. Bowker Company (annual).

Mogel, Leonard. *Making It in Publishing: An Insider's Guide to Career Opportunities*. New York, N.Y.: Macmillan, 1994.

Morgan, Bradley J., ed. *Book Publishing Career Directory*. Detroit, Mich.: Gale Research, Inc., 1993.

CHAPTER FOUR

Magazine and Newspaper Careers

Answering the Need for Information

F irst there were newspapers. Then magazines developed from newspapers. The reason for having magazines was to review books, while newspapers concentrated more on news. Both early magazines and newspapers looked much the same and were held together by folds. The difference was that newspapers had numerous folds, while magazines only had one. Because magazines fell apart easily, they were soon bound. Then most magazines and newspapers no longer looked alike.

While today some magazines and newspapers still may look the same, most magazines differ from newspapers in these obvious ways:

higher grade of paper

distinctive cover

more varied typeface

more color illustrations

different writing style

more white space

Both newspapers and magazines have many jobs that require considerable reading. By finding out more about what jobs are available at each of these publications, bookworms can decide which one is a better career fit for their personalities.

Becoming Better Acquainted with Magazines

Publications bound in paper covers that appear regularly and contain stories, articles, and illustrations by various contributors are usually called magazines. Magazines are also called periodicals, publications, journals, reviews, newsletters, and even books. So whenever you see one of these words in a want ad, you are looking at an advertisement for a job on a magazine.

Join the staff of a magazine and you are joining a long list of literary greats. Throughout the history of magazines, many well-known authors worked on magazine staffs, contributed articles to magazines, and even started magazines. You may be surprised to learn that Charles Dickens, Washington Irving, Oliver Wendell Holmes, Ralph Waldo Emerson, and Henry Adams were all involved in some way with magazines.

Newer Media Have Not Vanquished Magazines

Neither movies, television, nor VCRs have grabbed such a giant share of people's attention that magazines are no longer being read. In fact, today, more than 12,000 different magazines are being published in the United States. Furthermore, each year several hundred new magazines are started. In 1992, a record 679 new magazines were launched. Admittedly, it is a tough market to crack because only a handful last. Benjamin Franklin couldn't make it with his *General Magazine*. But in spite of all the competition, some new magazines, like *People*, for example, do succeed quite sensationally. At the same time, some prominent old magazines fold each year, as the 92-year-old *House and Garden* did in 1993.

Magazine sales are now at an all-time high. According to the *United States Industrial Outlook, 1994*, total magazine sales in 1994 will top more than $24 billion. With more than 120,000 people employed in magazine publishing, this is a good place for bookworms to look for jobs that involve reading.

Finding the Right Magazine for a Job

Just walk into any drugstore, bookstore, or even the grocery store and check out the magazine racks. It won't take longer than a few minutes to discover that there are magazines on almost any subject that you can think of, from coin collecting to family health. Most of these magazines fall into the category of consumer magazines. The other large category is trade, technical, and professional magazines. There are jobs for bookworms in both categories.

Consumer Magazines

More than 2,000 different consumer magazines are sold in the United States. Their circulation and revenue far exceed that of the greater number of trade, technical, and professional magazines. Approximately 150 of these magazines deal with general interests; the rest are devoted to specialized interests. Job seekers who want to work on magazines appealing to general interests usually have degrees in journalism or English. Obtaining a job on magazines with very large circulations can be quite competitive. Experience will count in getting one of these jobs.

On the other hand, if you want to work for a specialized consumer magazine, like one dealing with computers, needlework, motorcycles, crafts, dancing, or antiques, you definitely need some knowledge of that area. You are not going to get a job at a specialized computer magazine—an area that has more than 50 magazines—unless you know what bytes, bits, crashing, and control keys are. Nor will you be a good candidate for a job with a motorcycle magazine if you have never put on a helmet and ridden on a motorcycle. Being a bookworm can help you get a job with a specialized magazine if you have done in-depth reading in the area it covers. You can find lists of all the consumer magazines that are currently being published by looking at *Industrial Magazine Marketplace* or *SRDS (Standard Rate and Data Service) Consumer Magazine Directory*.

Trade, Technical, and Professional Magazines

You won't usually find trade, technical, and professional magazines on magazine racks. You might find one in a doctor's, lawyer's, or accountant's office because many of these publications deal with professions. Just think of any profession; there is probably one or more magazines dealing with that profession. The medical profession has a very impressive list of almost 500 magazines.

What do you think *Bank News*, *Boating Industry*, *Modern Tire Dealer*, and *Nuclear News* have in common? They bring information to people who are interested in what is happening in these industries. Scarcely an industry in the United States does not have a magazine. Advertising, tobacco, welding, railroads, textiles, travel, sewage disposal, coal mining, bicycles, and luggage all have magazines, to name just a few industries. If you are interested in a career in business magazines, make sure you look at the *SRDS* (*Standard Rate and Data Service*) *Business Magazine Directory* for a list of all the business magazines that are published. You also should know that several large companies publish more than one magazine. Some publish as many as 40 magazines.

To work on certain trade, technical, and professional magazines you are going to need academic training in a specific area. People working on medical magazines need to have a scientific background. In other areas, it helps to be knowledgeable about a particular profession or industry; but it is not always essential. You can learn about a profession or industry through on-the-job training. Fortunately, bookworms are employees who are willing to learn through reading.

Editorial Jobs at Magazines

Magazines are definitely good places for bookworms to look for work. Employees on the editorial side do a lot of reading. Perhaps, the better workplace for a bookworm is a consumer magazine or a magazine for a particular profession. More reading will occur at these magazines because most of the material is being written by outside authors or people within a profession. This means that articles and stories will have to be considered for acquisition and copyedited—both jobs that require considerable reading. If you work for a business magazine that publishes information about an industry, it is likely that you will be doing more writing than reading because many of these magazines are mainly written in-house.

When you think about working for a magazine, the size of the magazine really determines the kind of job that you are going to have. If you work for one of the giants in the magazine industry, your job will simply be in one specific area. Work for a magazine with a staff of 30 or 40 people, and your job description will be considerably broader. If you really want to be a jack-of-all-trades, get a job on a magazine that has an editorial staff of only one or two people.

The Pecking Order at Magazines

There really is not much difference between the organization charts of book publishing companies and most magazine publishers. The size of the magazine dictates how many different slots the editorial ladder will have. What an employee does at any job varies from one magazine to another.

Editor-in-Chief or Editor

Standing on the top rung of the ladder is the editor-in-chief, who is responsible for the editorial content of the magazine. A person in this position must delegate many responsibilities to other members of the staff.

Managing Editor

Reporting directly to the editor-in-chief, there is usually a managing editor or a group of associate or senior editors doing this job, which is to supervise the daily activities at the magazine. The managing editor's job also entails handling the staff and free-lance writers, as well as writing and editing personal projects. The larger the magazine, the greater the number of assistant editors reporting to the managing editor. Most managing editors come up through the editorial ranks.

The Other Editors

Depending on the size and organization of a magazine, you will find senior editors, associate editors, copyeditors, and assistant editors. Many of these editors are specialists in a certain field like fashion, travel, or politics, and may be called fashion editor, travel editor, political editor, or editor of whatever their specialty is. All of these editors do some reading; however, out of this group the copyeditor is the one doing the most reading.

Editorial Assistant

Editorial assistant is an entry-level position in which you not only learn about how a magazine is put out but also learn how to handle a variety of tasks from copyediting to acquisition.

Starting at the Bottom of the Ladder

With a recent degree in journalism in hand, Leigh Davis started her career working as an editorial assistant at the *Saturday Evening Post*. She regards this job as a great beginning for an eager bookworm. Leigh feels that it is difficult to get a job in magazine publishing and that more than a degree is needed. She has found that experience counts and thinks that her work on the college newspaper really helped her get this job. Even having worked on a high school newspaper staff would be helpful experience on a job seeker's résumé.

Leigh's beginning job on the editorial side of the magazine required a lot of reading. First of all, she spent a brief period of time every day reading through other general magazines to see what trends these magazines were following, especially in their travel sections.

Approximately one-third of Leigh's day was spent reading and researching as a fact checker. For example, after checking the facts on a travel story on South Padre Island, she researched for general information on barrier islands like South Padre Island. Then she added some of these facts to the travel story.

Another job that took a considerable portion of Leigh's time was reading unsolicited manuscripts. A select few were forwarded to editors as possibilities for later publication.

Copyediting, however, is what took up most of Leigh's time in this job. Not only did she have to read and proofread entire articles, she even had to do quite a bit of rewriting on them. What was left of Leigh's day was spent doing clerical tasks like sending manuscript guidelines to free-lance authors and responding to authors' questions about where their manuscripts were. Because the staff at the *Saturday Evening Post* was quite small, Leigh feels that she learned more than she would have in the same position at a larger magazine because she had the opportunity to work in more areas.

Letters Editor

Other jobs on magazine staffs require considerable reading. Bill Christophersen, letters editor at *Newsweek* magazine, has one of those jobs. Between 800 and 1,400 letters arrive at Newsweek magazine each week. Bill and his staff have the responsibility of handling this mail. After the letters are opened, a clerk determines where they will be routed. Some will be forwarded to other departments. The remaining letters are distributed to the staff of the letters department for reply. Staff members—many with master's degrees in journalism—answer all these letters.

A great number of the letters are routine and can be answered by form letters or slightly adapted form letters. Others require original replies, often necessitating some research. These letters must be accurate because they reflect the views of *Newsweek's* editors. The letters correspondents often need to consult with the author of an article for help in drafting a reply.

Each week one of the staff members sorts through all the letters and divides them into groups reflecting the stories they are commenting on and the viewpoints of the letter writers. Then Bill and one of his staff select the letters that will be used in the letters column of the magazine. Many letters have to be edited for reasons of clarity and space. Bill also adds editor's comments when necessary.

Bill believes that reading letters is an excellent way to start at *Newsweek*. Not only does this job have the fringe benefit that you might be noticed; it also provides valuable experience in editing, researching, and writing—skills essential to journalism. Before getting this job, it is necessary to pass a test demonstrating the ability to write clear conversational prose.

The Magazine Pay Scale

Starting out on the editorial side of the magazine industry will give you much the same income as starting in the book publishing industry. Most entry-level positions average slightly more than $20,000 a year. At all levels you will make more working for trade, technical, and professional magazines than at consumer magazines. You will also make more money at the same position at magazines with larger circulations. If you are working on a magazine in the Northeast, you will earn more than in any other region. It is also quite likely that you will be working in the area around New York City because that is the hub of the magazine industry. Unfortunately, it also costs more to live in this region.

Getting Your Foot in the Door

No one perfect route guarantees a job with a magazine. Certainly, a liberal arts degree seems to be a starting point for most people working on the editorial side of magazine publishing. Experience with a publication—from high school newspaper to college literary magazine—is also helpful. Even a little experience lets a prospective magazine employee write down something in the spaces asking for experience on application forms.

Having an internship on a magazine is an excellent way to get the experience job hunters need. Some internships are part-time jobs during the school year in which students receive academic credit and no money. There are also summer programs that offer some pay. You will find that most publishers have intern programs. These jobs are both for undergraduates and recent graduates. The reference section of the library has many directories listing internships. Before you sign up for an internship program, make sure that it is project-oriented and that you know exactly what you will be doing. Twelve weeks of meaningless clerical work could seem like an eternity. It can also be helpful to select an internship at a firm where you would later like to work.

Another avenue in preparing for a job in magazine publishing is attending a writing course during the summer. The oldest course is the Radcliffe/Harvard publishing program. Stanford University also has a program; however, it requires participants to have worked in the publishing industry for at least three years.

The First Steps as an Intern

Jennie Duffy, a recent college graduate in communications, wants to find a job on a weekly lifestyle magazine. She needs solid recommendations from an employer in this area, experience in working on a magazine, and samples of her work to show prospective employers. Jennie hopes to fill these needs through a three-month internship with Diablo Publications working on the firm's *Diablo Magazine*, a lifestyle magazine in northern California. As an intern, she has been able to do some writing and is also spending time researching and fact checking. Because the internship only pays a modest stipend, Jennie has two other jobs in order to support herself. Nevertheless, Jennie is optimistic that she is on the way to a career with a magazine.

Your Future in the Magazine Industry

Circulation is holding steady in the magazine industry, and publishers are working hard to hold on to their readers. Special interest magazines are becoming increasingly popular as they target readers' specific interests—from regional travel to organic gardening. Expect many new magazines in areas geared to families, teenagers, sports lovers, and other hobbyists. These narrowly targeted magazines are looking for individuals who can produce a high-quality product. Perhaps, this is where you will find a job on a magazine. Also, the demand for technical writers is expected to increase because of the continuing expansion of scientific and technical information and the continued need to communicate it in a readable style in various magazines.

Becoming Better Acquainted with Newspapers

The first printed newspaper, the *Dibao*, was published during the eighth century in China. Even earlier, newspapers were hand-written and posted in public places. One of these was the *Acta Diurna*, meaning Daily Events, which actually started in Rome in 59 B.C.

Benjamin Harris of Boston founded the first newspaper in the United States in 1690. It was called the *Publick Occurrences Both Forreign and Domestick* and had an extraordinarily brief history because the government stopped it after the first issue. The 1800s were the heyday for the development of newspapers. The largest number of newspapers ever in the United States was about 2,600 dailies in 1909. Today, the number of daily newspapers is less than 1,600. Although overall circulation is increasing for daily papers, it's a mixed picture. Morning circulation is increasing, and evening circulation is dropping. Furthermore, some major metropolitan newspapers are losing circulation to the growing number of suburban newspapers. There are also 6,600 weekly newspapers, whose circulation is steadily expanding.

See if you can identify the three newspapers with the largest circulation today from the following list:

Wall Street Journal

New York Times

Detroit Free Press

Boston Globe

Los Angeles Times

Miami Herald

U.S.A. Today

Minneapolis Star Tribune

Your first choice should have been the *Wall Street Journal* followed by *U.S.A. Today* and the *New York Times*.

Falling circulation is not the only reason newspapers fail. The money that you put in a newspaper box or pay the carrier does not cover the cost of the labor and materials involved in producing the paper. Just like the magazine industry, the money to run newspapers comes mainly from advertising sales.

The U.S.A. *Today* Story

In the few years since it first hit the newsstands on September 16, 1982, U.S.A. *Today* has become the second largest newspaper in terms of circulation and the largest in terms of readership. More than 6 million people read U.S.A. *Today* five days a week. In 1994, the newspaper employed 2,100 people at 32 print sites. This paper is the first and only national, daily, general-interest newspaper in the United States.

Climbing to the Top

The climb to the top in the newspaper publishing industry is very similar to the book and magazine industries. Dennis Hetzel is a bookworm who has gone from writing for a local paper in high school to being the editor and publisher of the *Daily Record* in York, Pennsylvania.

Starting out in Newspaper Publishing

Dennis began his newspaper career in high school. Not being able to excel in sports, Dennis coupled his love of sports with his writing ability to write about sports for the local weekly. He majored in political science and minored in journalism in college and had plans to become a high school teacher—he even did his student teaching. However, an opportunity to become the sports editor for two weekly papers changed his career path. He believes that it was his high school experience that got him this job. Working in sports, according to Dennis, requires a tremendous amount of reading each day just to keep track of what is happening in sports.

After a year, Dennis went to another paper in Galesburg, Illinois, as a reporter. On this paper, one of his beats was the courts. This job required an ability to read fast and to read for understanding. Dennis had to look at lengthy, complicated documents and figure out what the important points were.

Starting to Climb the Editorial Ladder

After going to another paper in Racine, Wisconsin, as a reporter, within a few years Dennis became special projects editor at that paper. He did a lot of research on this job; he read and edited others' work and researched special projects. Continuing his upward climb, Dennis became an associate editor. This job required him to supervise the copy desk and do the front page. He had to read stories coming in from outside news services and pick out the ones to use in the paper. Several hundred stories might be available, while there was room for only a few dozen.

Managing Editor

In 1986, Dennis became managing editor of the *Capital Times* in Madison, Wisconsin. Half or more of his time was spent on managerial tasks. He read and wrote a lot of memos, but he also read newspapers and articles in trade magazines like *Editor and Publisher*. Besides reading his own newspaper, he read two or three other newspapers every morning and an afternoon newspaper.

Editor and Publisher

In 1990, Dennis became the editor and publisher of the *Daily Record*. As publisher, he is the chief operating officer and also plays more of a role in community affairs. As editor, he is responsible for setting the overall policy and direction of the newspaper. Much of his reading today is concentrated on learning more about the information highway and where we are headed. Dennis still reads several newspapers a day; however, he finds that he is reading more on-line and sees a migration away from print. He believes that it is absolutely essential to read in order to succeed in the newspaper industry. This should be good news for bookworms.

Copyediting Means Reading All Day

For many bookworms, copyediting may seem like the perfect job. It requires on-the-job reading—not for just part of the day, but all day each and every workday. Copyediting is the process of reviewing and editing the work of reporters so it is ready to be set in type. It involves finding and correcting spelling, grammar, and punctuation errors. Copyediting on a magazine or a book may involve fact checking, but copy is generally considered to be correct on newspapers. There just isn't time on a newspaper for fact checking beyond looking for obvious errors or inconsistencies. Bookworms have to realize that copyeditors do not sit in soft easy chairs leisurely doing their editing. At most newspapers, they sit in front of computers staring at stories on monitors for hours. Furthermore, the pace is quite fast as they hurry to get copy ready to be printed. Perhaps one of the best ways to determine if copyediting is the job for you is to read about what a copyediting job on a large metropolitan newspaper with a circulation of more than 100,000 involves.

The Copyeditor's Job

L.T. Brown is one of 12 copyeditors at the *Indianapolis News*. At the start of the day, 30 or 40 stories may be stored in the newspaper's computer system waiting to be edited. Reporters have written the stories and given them to their editors, who may have made some changes. The editors also have placed instructions on the stories detailing what kind of headlines are to be used and what the size of the story should be (column length and width). These stories are then sent to the slot man—the editor who parcels out assignments and makes sure that the copyeditors are working on what is needed. All this is done by computer on most newspapers.

L.T. tries to choose stories that interest him and to avoid those written by sloppy reporters. He pulls a story up on his computer monitor, and the copyediting process begins. According to journalism textbooks, stories should be read through completely before copyediting begins. With the time restraints of newspaper deadlines, this just doesn't happen too much of the time. As L.T. reads through the copy, he edits. For an experienced copyeditor, like L.T., the errors usually jump out. He knows what words are always misspelled and even what mistakes individual reporters make. At times, he must do considerable rewriting to meet space specifications, which are so tight that he may substitute the word "try" for "attempt." By the press of a button on his computer, L.T. can tell whether the story is the correct length or not. When a story is the correct size, L.T. writes the headline according to the instructions. The story is then sent to the slot man, who glances through it and sends it to typesetting.

When the first edition of the paper comes out, L.T. and the other copyeditors read through it, and note any needed corrections on the paper. New stories in subsequent editions are also checked for errors. All corrections are given to the slot man.

Personal Qualifications of Copyeditors

You must have a love affair with words. You should enjoy playing with words. Most copyeditors are confirmed punsters. They also work crosswords, as L.T. does, to learn smaller words for larger words. Above all, you need to be a bookworm who enjoys reading a wide variety of material both on and off the job. Your academic background will probably consist of a bachelor's degree in journalism or English.

The Newspaper Pay Scale

Whether your first job is working for a book publisher, a magazine publisher, or a newspaper, you will not be earning a high starting salary. Although some reporters work on union newspapers that negotiate their salaries with the Newspaper Guild, most don't. In 1994, the range of salaries for reporters stretched from a very low $245 per week for some beginning reporters to $1,269 per week for top reporters on major newspapers. Copyeditors usually receive comparable salaries to reporters.

Getting Your Foot in the Door

You are most likely to get your first job in the newspaper industry because a reporter or correspondent has left the industry, been promoted, or moved to a larger newspaper. Competition for jobs on major newspapers is fierce. Small town and suburban papers offer better opportunities for finding that all-important first job. No matter where you get your first job, you are likely to be working for a newspaper chain because 76 percent of all newspapers are owned by chains.

To get just about any entry-level job on a newspaper, you will be expected to have excellent word-processing skills. Computer graphics and desktop publishing skills may also be useful. Most employers will expect you to have a bachelor's degree in journalism, but some hire graduates with other majors. Experience is very important in getting a job. It is just about essential to be able to list an internship, part-time job, or summer job in the industry to secure your first newspaper job. It even helps to have worked on your high school or college newspaper.

Your Future in the Newspaper Industry

While newspapers are forecast to grow in the 1990s, greater emphasis will be placed on delivering readers the specific information that they want. Like books and magazines, newspapers will explore the delivery of information in electronic as well as print form.

For bookworms, newspapers are an appealing career choice. Of course, not every employee reads for 8 hours a day, but most do some reading. Furthermore, positions like copyeditor and wire editor offer almost 8 hours a day of reading. The newspaper industry has more than 400,000 employees, which is almost four times the number of people employed by the magazine industry. Perhaps, you will be one of these employees in the future.

Two Satisfying Careers for Bookworms

What do people working on magazines and newspapers have in common? They almost always love their work. They thrive on the excitement of deadlines, whether they are the deadlines for different editions of a newspaper or the weekly, monthly, or quarterly deadlines of magazines. They universally complain about low pay. They garner satisfaction from providing information so that people can know what is going on around them. But most of all, they savour working with words in some way. For undeniably, jobs on both magazines and newspapers offer considerable opportunity to read.

For Further Reading

Because so many opportunities exist for employment in magazine and newspaper publishing, it is a good idea to look at directories that list the large number of companies in this field. All kinds of interesting job possibilities exist. You might find it possible to combine your interest in birds or clothing with working on a consumer specialty magazine. Perhaps, your addiction to reading about current events would be satisfied through working on a newspaper. You should find information in the following books to be helpful:

Directories

Bacon's Magazine Directory. Chicago, Ill.: Bacon's Information Inc.
Bacon's Newspaper Directory. Chicago, Ill.: Bacon's Information Inc.
The Directory of Small Press & Magazine Editors & Publishers. Paradise, Calif.: Dustbooks.

A Guide to Publishing and Bookselling Courses in the U.S. Princeton, N.J.:
    Peterson's Guides, 1992.
Morgan, Bradley J., ed. *Magazines Career Directory.* Detroit, Mich.: Gale
    Research Inc., 1993.
———. *Newspapers Career Directory.* Detroit, Mich.: Gale Research Inc., 1993.
The Standard Periodical Directory. New York, N.Y.: Oxbridge Communications,
    Inc.
Troshynski, Karen, Deborah M. Burek, and Thomas Burek. *Gale Directory of
    Publications and Broadcast Media.* Detroit, Mich.: Gale Research Inc.

Career Books

Berner, R. Thomas. *The Process of Writing News.* Needham Heights, Mass.:
    Allyn, 1992.
Mann, Jim. *Magazine Editing: Its Art and Practice.* Stamford, Conn.: Hanson
    Publishing Group, Inc., 1985.
Mogel, Leonard. *The Magazine: Everything You Need to Know to Make It in the
    Magazine Business.* Old Saybrook, Conn.: The Globe Pequot Press, 1992.
Pattis, S. William. *Opportunities in Magazine Publishing Careers.* Lincolnwood,
    Ill.: NTC Publishing Group, 1992.
Tebbel, John. *Opportunities in Newspaper Publishing Careers.* Lincolnwood, Ill.:
    NTC Publishing Group, 1989.

CHAPTER FIVE

Glamourous Careers
Reading in the Limelight

W hy would anyone ever want to work at a job that requires long and hard hours, offers low pay for years, and does not have a great deal of job security? The answer is simple—the job is a glamourous one. It probably involves working in radio, television, movies, or public relations. The lure of working in these areas is so great that college graduates are fiercely competing for entry level positions. After all, even jobs starting at the bottom offer the chance to answer a superstar's mail, critique a script that goes on to become a television or movie blockbuster, or do research for a talk show host. And many of the entry-level jobs like the ones just mentioned involve considerable reading. What's more, there are jobs further up the glamour career ladder that are perfect for bookworms.

Preparation for entering a glamour industry job is just up a bookworm's alley. You simply have to read as much as you can to get an idea of the basics of how radio and television shows are produced, movies are made, and public relations campaigns are handled.

Radio—The Vocal Medium

Many people don't realize that before television became so popular families sat around their radios every evening. They listened to "Great Gildersleeve," "The Jack Benny Program,"

67

and "Inner Sanctum Mysteries" for entertainment. They found out about what was happening in the world by listening to Lowell Thomas, Edward R. Murrow, and other famous news commentators. Some danced to the music of the big bands or top forty tunes. But this golden age of radio ended when television took over these roles.

Radio did not roll over and play dead. Instead, radio changed its format. All-talk, all-news, and all-music stations emerged, as well as stations with formats designed to attract a particular audience. Soon radio had captured more listeners than ever before. In fact, homes today have a far greater number of radios than television sets. Perhaps, part of this can be traced to the convenience of radio. You can drive a car and listen to the radio. You can jog down the street listening to a radio. You can listen to radios on buses, trains, and ferris wheels. The current popularity of radio means more jobs for people wanting to work in this medium. Many of these jobs are designed for people who love to talk and read.

Radio Deejays Read

Jeff Pigeon is a radio deejay on an adult contemporary program at WIBC in Indianapolis. Jeff is an early morning bookworm—not a 24 hour-a-day bookworm. Arriving at the station every morning at 4:15 A.M. for his 5:00 A.M. show, he begins reading immediately. He reads the local morning paper plus two other newspapers so he will know what has been happening locally and around the world when he goes on the air. His producer is also busily reading and giving Jeff highlighted articles to take into the studio.

While Jeff enjoys reading, he is definitely not a speed reader. Because he likes to take his time with the printed word and slowly absorb what he is reading, he does a lot of his reading at home. He always reads the evening paper along with a whole list of popular magazines, and even the tabloids. Jeff is also kept busy trying to keep up with all the new books that publishers send to him. He has to resort to skimming many of these books.

Jeff is constantly preparing for his show. Everything that happens to him during the day as well as anything he reads could be a good topic of conversation on one of his shows. He feels that those who want to succeed in the radio industry will read as much material as they can get their hands on.

Talk Show Stars and Producers Read

You have probably listened to talk shows and may even have called in to offer your opinion on some topic. Many radio stations have an all-talk format with jobs for bookworms as show hosts or producers. Here are two jobs where you absolutely must read in order to know what is going on in the world, whether you are Rush Limbaugh talking politics or the host on the local station discussing with callers what is happening in your community.

Patty Stanton is producer of the "Ronn Owens Show," which airs five mornings a week on KGO in San Francisco. This is a very popular news talk show that has people call in. Ronn, the host, interacts with the callers and also interviews guests. He is an avid reader, and so is Patty. Because Ronn's show airs in the morning, Patty regularly gets up at 4:30 A.M. so she can go through eight newspapers. With a solid knowledge of what has been going on in the world, Patty is ready to give her input on the list of topics for the show to Ronn. Part of her job also involves reading newspapers and magazines to look for good guests, as well as moral issues for Ronn's personal opinion segment at the start of the show. During the show, she screens calls looking for people with passion and divergent views to bring balance to the show. After the show, she discusses the next day's program with Ronn. She also selects books and mail for him to read. Because she has so much reading to do for her job as producer, Patty is still reading a book she started two months ago.

Movies—A Glamourous Environment for Readers

The movie industry is a rather small one, with fewer than 250,000 people working in it. If your dream is to work in this industry, you should pack your bags and head for southern

California because it's still the center of moviemaking. Most of the movie jobs that are ideal for bookworms center on handling scripts. Some jobs will put you in touch with the stars—from handling their fan mail to reading scripts for them. Some jobs also exist in doing research to determine that everything shown in a film is as authentic as possible. Whatever your job in this industry, the possibility of meeting famous stars and directors is always there.

The movie industry is a close-knit one. Getting a job seems to be tied to knowing someone who has a job or knows about a job. The secret in finding the job you want often lies in taking an entry-level job that will let you make contacts in the industry and will also acquaint you with the different types of jobs available. Reading also helps. Through reading *Variety* and *The Hollywood Reporter*, two dailies on the movie industry, you can find out what is happening in every phase of the industry from new film stars to movies currently in production.

A Possible Starting Point

There is a rumor that Woody Allen started as a script typist. Whether this is true or not, the job is one that gives you a look at a lot of scripts. Being a script typist is excellent preparation for becoming a story analyst or a screenwriter. After you have handled hundreds of scripts, you will learn what is good and thoroughly understand the format in which scripts are written.

According to Valerie Koutnik, who was a script typist in Hollywood and is now a screenwriter, the job involves taking a script and putting it into the correct format. There are many complex rules for the layout of dialogue and descriptive passages, with different styles for film and television.

The two basic requirements for getting a job as a script typist are: (1) you must be an excellent typist; (2) you must be a person who will safeguard the confidentiality of the scripts you type. Just think of how important script confidentiality was when J.R. was shot on "Dallas."

Valerie believes that a significant advantage of script-typing work is that it is one of the easier ways to get inside the film industry. Script typists can find work with independent production companies, studios, artists' agencies, free-lance writers, and professional script-typing companies. You can find script-typing companies listed in the Los Angeles yellow pages. Although the pay is hourly and the work can sometimes be tedious, she feels it is invaluable experience in seeing how scripts are put together.

Working as a Story Analyst

Working as a story analyst or as a reader, which is another name for the same job, is ideal for a bookworm. The job involves reading movie scripts, books, and plays to find one that will make a movie that will earn money. The whole industry is searching for these movies, so there are jobs at agencies, studios, production companies, and with individual stars. To work at most studios you have to belong to a union for story analysts. There are many places where you can read without belonging to this union as well as many opportunities to be a free-lancer. A free-lancer can earn from $10 to $15 at the low end of the scale to $40 to $50 at the high end for reading each script. The pay range is from $60 to $200 for books and longer-than usual scripts.

The Job Description

Story analysts read movie scripts, books, and plays, and write coverages. Each studio, production company, or agency will use a different form for coverages, which involve the following three things:

1. A *synopsis* is written that retells the story as clearly as possible. The length and detail of the synopsis vary with the story analyst's employer.

2. The story analyst's *opinion* is given explaining whether or not the story has commercial value, is castable, and is similar to other movies or well-known books.

3. A *rating scale* is usually filled in that rates such things as production value, structure, characterization, and dialogue on a scale from poor to excellent.

Job Qualifications Needed

No degree is required for the job of story analyst. However, the analyst should have developed a literary sense from a lot of reading and a visual sense from having seen a lot of movies. Story analysts also need to know how to write.

Getting a Job as a Story Analyst

With a degree in film, radio, and television in hand, Randy Kornfield entered the job market with the desire to become a screenwriter. A friend got him a part-time job duplicating scripts at a studio. Then he was promoted to the mailroom. During this time he was meeting people and deciding where he wanted to work, as well as trying to write screenplays. A move to another studio brought Randy a job as a secretary and assistant in personnel. At this job, he met a story editor who let him read some scripts and write coverages. This gave him the chance to see what good and bad scripts were like, as well as what kind of scripts were being bought. When this job folded, Randy became a free-lance story analyst. Then he found a job at another studio as an assistant to an executive who was looking for scripts. At this job, which was primarily secretarial, he was able to read some scripts but didn't have to write coverages. After management changes at the studio, Randy was out of a job again. He next found a job as a story analyst at a nonunion studio. Then he was able to get a story analyst job at MGM, a union studio, because the story editor whom he met earlier was now working at this studio. The advantage of working at a union studio is better pay plus benefits. Unforunately, it is very difficult to get in the story analyst union.

During all this time, Randy was busy writing and actually sold a screenplay and had a low-budget movie made from one of his scripts. Reading scripts has been helpful in his writing. Today, Randy is working at 20th Century Fox as a story analyst and still writing in his spare time. His writing success continues. He has had two more movies produced on television.

Story Analyst for a Movie Star

Would you like to talk to a movie star on the phone or perhaps have him or her come to your office several times a week? All of this is part of Sandy Erickson's job as a story analyst. She reads scripts and books looking for the right properties for Matt Dillon. This is a glamour job that lets Sandy read 70 percent of the time. You can find jobs like hers in the offices of managers and agents of movie stars.

Reading Fan Mail

Movie stars gets loads of letters from their fans. Almost all of this mail is handled by a fan club service provided by a star's manager, agent, or studio. Most of the letters are from people simply requesting pictures. The rest of the letters can usually be answered by form letters. Only a few letters require a personal reply.

Running a Production Company

This is a glamorous job, yet Matt Levy reads 50 percent of the time while running Kiefer Sutherland's production company at 20th Century Fox. Matt spends much of his day searching for the right property for Kiefer to act in, produce, or direct. This involves reading a lot of scripts and books as well as newspapers and magazines for ideas. Matt also meets with writers and listens to pitches—all to find possibilities for Kiefer's consideration.

Many actors have someone who reads for them because they don't have the time to evaluate all the materials out there when they are working. There are literally hundreds of ways to get these jobs—from starting in the mailroom and building relations with people in the industry to working with an actor on a movie as Matt did with Kiefer. When you land a job like this, you may find yourself employed by a very eccentric actor, or you may be as lucky as Matt and find yourself working for someone very pleasant. In any case, there is lots of competition for these jobs.

Television—Almost Everyone's Favorite Medium

In the United States, television sets are found in more than 95 percent of the homes, and these sets are on for an average of more than 6 hours a day. From the crack of dawn until late at night, there are many households where the television set is rarely off. People can be totally entertained right in their own homes just by turning on their television sets. They can find whatever interests them, whether it is movies, quiz shows, soap operas, cartoons, educational programs, situation comedies, action-packed dramas, variety shows, news shows, or sports events. What is significant to the jobseeker is that each show requires more people behind the scenes than the ones seen on the television screen. And many of these jobs both on-camera and off-camera are good choices for bookworms who want jobs that require considerable reading.

Network Story Editor

DeNece Gilbert knew that she wanted to work for a large television network even before she graduated from college with a communications degree. So after graduation she headed west— straight for Hollywood. Not knowing anyone and without any experience, she couldn't get a job in television. She did get a job in the publishing division of Motown Records; the job required her to place songs with the appropriate Motown artist.

After gaining experience at Motown, DeNece became a secretary at a major network. Several promotions later, she was the assistant to the director of comedy and drama. This job was a bookworm's delight. DeNece's job was to read scripts and treatments and to write a one-page synopsis of each work for the director. She worked on the weekly episodes of such popular shows as "Magnum, P.I." "Dallas," "Dukes of Hazard," and "All in the Family."

Today, DeNece is working for a major network in New York City as a story editor covering books. It is her job to find books that would make good television movies or miniseries. She works with 30 large publishing houses in New York and 30 other smaller publishing houses throughout the country. Her only job is to look for a good story. DeNece does not do any writing or rewriting. The network hires writers or uses in-house writers for any changes or adaptations that are needed.

On the job, most of DeNece's reading time is spent going through publishing catalogs. She usually orders 10 or 11 books from each catalog. DeNece also looks through the *Kirkus Review*, which lists upcoming books, and *Publishers Weekly*. She reads popular consumer magazines as well as newspapers to discover future trends. She usually takes manuscripts and books home to read so that she can read them without interruption.

DeNece can't read everything, so she has ten free-lance readers who keep busy reading for her. Readers receive approximately $75 for a book and $35 for a screenplay. They write a two-and-one-half page summary of the material and a one-page personal comment sheet. If a free-lancer suggests a second reading or praises the work, DeNece will read the material.

It takes more than one year from the time material goes into development until it is seen on the air. DeNece looks for fresh work and often goes for first-time authors like Chris Bohjalian, who wrote *A Killing in the Real World*. His book was adapted into a television play called "Deadly Reunion".

Glamour does enter into this ideal job for a bookworm. The casting office is right next to DeNece's office. There are trips to the large book fairs and the Louisville Playwriter's Festival. At this festival, she is not only looking at the plays but is also on the lookout for good new writers.

According to DeNece, networks have many other jobs that bookworms would like. Script readers are needed for every division in a network. For the children's afterschool specials, the readers even read children's books to find new program ideas. There are also jobs for research librarians.

Segment Producers and Producers of Talk Shows

All those talk shows you see on television have producers. Some even have producers for each segment of the show. These producers are responsible for what happens on a show—a job usually requiring considerable reading.

A talk show producer may read the books of authors who are going to be on the program and then frame questions for the talk show host. Then there are all the books that land on the talk show producer's desk; these must be looked at to see which authors should be selected to appear on the program. Research may also be done on each guest on the program to acquaint the host with the day's guest or guests. Furthermore, there is the task of keeping up with what is happening in the world so provocative guests and subjects can be chosen. A daily talk show consumes a lot of material, so the search for new ideas is never-ending. Most of these ideas will evolve from the reading done by the show's producer or producers.

Jobs as producers and segment producers are not usually entry-level jobs except at smaller television stations. To be a producer of a major network show requires previous experience. A producer might start at a station as an assistant, advance to associate producer, and then be a coordinating producer before becoming a producer.

A News Show Producer

Producers of talk shows aren't the only ones who read. Producers of news shows also must read. Faye De Hoff produces the early evening "News Center Four at Five" show for the NBC affiliate in San Francisco. This is a prime-time half-hour news show that is aired Monday through Friday. The show deals mainly with local and national news of the day. After the top news stories have aired, the stories are geared toward medicine, women, children, and other topics appropriate for the time slot's audience.

Producers like Faye do considerable reading. Before work, she has read the local morning papers, and she will keep reading AP wire service material all day long to keep herself constantly updated on what is happening in the world. She must have this knowledge as she decides the editorial content of the news show. Faye is also busy determining the order in which stories will be presented on the show, the look of the show, the graphics that will be used, the use of live shots, and the myriad details that guarantee a smooth production.

Faye is a true bookworm. A recent trip to London and Scotland inspired her to read *Mary Queen of Scots* to keep the trip fresh in her mind. Quite often, seeing a movie will entice her to read the original book. Her nightstand always has a stack of books on it. She will go back and forth between two books at the same time and has been known to read a book in a night.

Producing a news show is not just reading. Faye does loads of writing for the program. Writing for television is quite different from writing for other media. The language must be simple and so must the sentences. On her show, the writing must be for the ear because many people at this time in the evening are viewing her show while doing other things.

News Reporters Need to Read

If you write the scripts for your news reports on television, then you will need to read for information. You simply can't do an in-depth treatment of a topic without having background information on it. To keep abreast of what is going on in the world for his job as a television news reporter for an NBC affiliate, David MacAnally reads daily papers, including the *New York Times*, plus news feature magazines.

News Anchor on a Midwest Station

Maybe some anchors are just performers. However, Tom Cochrun, evening news anchor at an NBC station in Indianapolis, is not one of them. Tom is a true bookworm who as a child stayed up many evenings with a flashlight trying to finish sports adventure books that got him hooked on reading.

In his job as news anchor, Tom reads for 60 to 80 percent of his workday. He reads newspapers, research reports, background reports, and magazines. Tom feels that in order to write news copy that his viewers will understand he has to have a strong grasp of the information. He says he cannot get this understanding from just reading wire service information. David Brinkley, Tom Brokaw, and Ted Koppel are other anchors who do a great deal of reading to prepare for their shows.

Public Relations

Companies, institutions, unions, activist groups, and all kinds of organizations want to win public approval. The people who do this job for them are in the public relations field, which is commonly called PR. Some organizations have their own public relations departments while others use public relations firms. In either case, the task is to communicate with a specific audience. Airlines may want to stress how safe it is to fly after several crashes have shaken the public's confidence in air travel. A chemical company may want to reassure its workers on the safety of the workplace. A food company may want to communicate to its stockholders the reasons why the price of its stock is steadily rising.

People employed in public relations work have two main activities: research and communication. Most of the glamour lies in the communication side because PR people arrange for media publicity. It is the research side that allows bookworms to read. In order to handle an account, it is essential to be well versed in what a client does. This may mean not only reading about a company but also an entire industry. The majority of reading is probably done to find out what newspapers and magazines are writing about clients. It is also important to gather information that may affect a client. Today's public relations employees are voracious readers who must read everything in order to service their clients effectively.

Travel Agents

The type of reading that travel agents do is frequently investigative. Cynthia Kroos, the managing director of a travel agency, finds it essential to learn about new tourist spots, resorts, and tours. She is constantly reading trade publications to do this. Obviously, a lot of reading also has to be done to keep up with all the packages that are offered by airlines and tour companies. According to Cynthia, travel agents have so much reading to do that it can almost bury them. Because so much of the workday is devoted to dealing with clients, considerable reading must be done at home. The glamorous bonus to all of this reading is the frequent trips that Cynthia takes to learn more about places her clients may wish to visit.

Reading Can Be Glamourous

While a glamour career may be appealing to many people, including bookworms, it is not easy to break into a glamourous field. Even college graduates are usually required to begin in low-level positions because experience is needed for the positions they seek. Few have that experience, so graduates are often forced to begin as secretaries, typists, or gofers to gain experience. There is always room for good people in glamour industries. However, getting the job of your dreams involves hard work as well as some luck and good timing.

Glamour careers at all levels can be pressure-filled and tension-packed as people struggle to meet deadlines for such things as television shows, advertising promotions, and the production of movies. There is no guarantee of a nine-to-five job. Like all careers, considerable drudgery is involved. However, glamour careers do offer involvement in exciting industries like radio, television, the movies, travel, advertising, and public relations, which makes these careers so sought after.

For Further Reading

The more you know about the glamour industries, the easier it will be for you to discover the job you want. A surprising number of jobs in this industry are filled by people who read for a substantial period of time each day. While most bookworms are working behind the scenes in these industries, a few are also in the public eye. The following books should give you a better idea of what careers are available in the glamour industries:

Bone, Jan. *Opportunities in Film Careers.* Lincolnwood, Ill.: NTC Publishing Group, 1990.
Ellis, Elmo I. *Opportunities in Broadcasting Careers.* Lincolnwood, Ill.: NTC Publishing Group, 1994.
Grant, Edgar. *Exploring Careers in the Travel Industry.* New York, N.Y.: The Rosen Publishing Group, Inc., 1989.
Greenspon, Jaq. *Careers for Film Buffs & Other Hollywood Types.* Lincolnwood, Ill.: NTC Publishing Group, 1994.

Mogel, Leonard. *Making it in Broadcasting: An Insider's Guide to Career Opportunities*. New York, N.Y.: Macmillan, 1994.

———. *Making it in Public Relations: An Insider's Guide to Career Opportunities*. New York, N.Y.: Macmillan, 1994.

Morgan, Bradley J. and Joseph M. Palmisano, eds. *Film and Video Career Directory*. Detroit, Mich.: Gale Research Inc., 1994.

Noronha, Shonan. *Opportunities in Television and Video Careers*. Lincolnwood, Ill.: NTC Publishing Group, 1994.

Reed, Maxine K. and Robert M. Reed. *Career Opportuiities in Television, Cable and Video*. New York, N.Y.: Facts on File Publications, 1991.

CHAPTER SIX

Education Careers
Sharing Knowledge

Books are the quietest and most constant of friends; they are the most accessible and wisest of counselors, and the most patient of teachers. CHARLES W. ELIOT

Teaching is a profession for bookworms. As the quote by Eliot, president of Harvard University from 1869 to 1909 and a pioneer in teacher education, clearly states books themselves are teachers. In order to teach, teachers from elementary school through college must love books, read books, and understand them. Books are an integral part of teaching. However, being a bookworm is not enough to make someone a good teacher. Good teachers must also be able to pass the knowledge, skills, and information that they have acquired from books on to their students.

Preparing Yourself to Teach

Teaching is not a new profession. Scholars like Aristotle, Plato, and Socrates were teachers. But it was not until the 1800s that teaching schools began to develop. Today, anyone planning to teach, whether in a kindergarten or at the college level, will need a college degree. Many elementary, junior high, and high school teachers will also need to get master's degrees to advance in the profession and to increase their earnings. Bookworms who want to teach at the college level will find it is very helpful to have a doctorate degree. Prospective elementary, junior high, and senior high school teachers will study similar courses during their first two years of college. These courses are basic liberal arts courses and will include the study of history, language arts, mathematics, and science. During their college years, they will also take teaching methods courses and do actual practice teaching in a classroom under the guidance of an experienced teacher. In addition, future high school teachers will also specialize in the particular subject area or areas in which they plan to teach.

Before most bookworms can start teaching, they will need to meet state requirements for teacher certification. These requirements deal with the college courses that teachers must complete satisfactorily to become certified elementary, junior, and senior high school teachers. Each state has different requirements. In some states teachers at nursery schools, private schools, and junior colleges also have to be certified. However, teachers at four-year colleges and universities do not need state certification.

Generic Teaching Duties

All teachers, no matter what level they are teaching, have a number of duties that must be performed—from taking attendance to filling out report cards.

Getting Ready

Bookworms will find preparation for classroom work enjoyable because it involves so much reading. Teachers read textbooks, teacher's manuals, course-related materials, professional journals, and curriculum guides to prepare for their daily stint in the classroom. However, preparation goes beyond reading to making sure everything is completely ready for each lesson. Materials have to be duplicated. Supplementary books and materials as well as supplies have to be obtained and laid out in readiness for each class.

Leading the Way

Teachers are the classroom leaders. Through a variety of different teaching methods, they have to motivate their students to learn, show them how to learn, and instill intellectual curiosity in them. Books will help them in this task, so will all kinds of audiovisual materials like records, tapes, filmstrips, movies, and television programs plus computers.

Checking Progress

All teachers need to make sure that their students have learned the material. Mastery is important, whether it is the alphabet, the multiplication tables, or French grammar. Teachers check their students' progress through analyzing written and oral work and quizzes and tests. Records need to be kept so that teachers know how each individual student is doing. And this information must be placed on report cards and discussed at conferences.

Being a Role Model

Students do notice how their teachers behave. Younger students, especially, often want to be just like their teachers. Teachers set a very powerful example for their students through their own sincerity, patience, kindness, understanding, honesty, and objectivity. Furthermore, teachers who truly love to read inspire their students to become lifelong readers.

Doing the Extra Tasks

Teachers have other obligations besides routine classroom tasks. They are also expected to do their share of duties such as supervising the lunchroom and bus loading, and hall and playground duty. They chaperone after-school events, attend faculty meetings, and sponsor clubs. Don't consider teaching as a profession if you expect to be home by 3 o'clock each day.

A Closer Look at the Teaching Profession

Today, education is both America's largest business and profession. There are more than 3 million teachers in the United States, and more than $1 billion is spent on education every school day in this country. The good news for people interested in this profession is that the number of students attending school will increase, which raises the demand for teachers. The demand for secondary school teachers will be especially strong because student enrollment is growing fastest at this level.

Teaching at the Lower Elementary Level

For bookworms, teaching children in the lower elementary grades can be very satisfying. These teachers have the opportunity to actually teach young children how to read and to help each child develop an appreciation for books. It is a chance for bookworms to instill their love of books in others.

According to Fran Hageboeck, a first-grade teacher for many years, half of her teaching day is devoted to some aspect of teaching reading. During that time, she will read outloud to the class for 30 minutes. Time is also spent having children read to her and listening to them read to each other. Away from the classroom, she spends time in the library searching for books to read to the children and for them to read.

Of course, first-grade teachers also teach other subjects beside reading. In addition, they spend time tying shoes, buttoning coats, putting on boots, and handing out tissues. But reading is the main focus of all the learning activities in first grade.

Teaching at the Upper Elementary Level

If you were turned off by the need to tie shoes and button coats at the lower elementary level but still like children, you might find it more enjoyable to teach in one of the upper elementary grades. In fourth, fifth, and sixth grades students can handle all their own personal needs and have also mastered the basic reading skills. Teachers at these grade levels are helping students become independent learners. Besides classes in reading and mathematics, students are now beginning to learn in the content areas of history, science, health, and English. For bookworms, it is an opportunity to help children expand their horizons through a broad reading program.

The trend today is to teach thematic units in which students study a topic like California and learn about its history, geography, and geology throughout the day as they study social studies, language arts, science, and mathematics. Searching for materials to use in this approach has Karen McCall, a fourth-grade teacher, reading avidly. Then to keep up with what is happening in her profession, she reads newsletters and professional journals. Finally, she reads local papers and periodicals to keep abreast of community happenings. For Karen, reading plays an important role in the quality of instruction she brings to the classroom.

Teaching at the Junior High Level

Sue Engledow, a true bookworm, made a career change from being a bank manager to being a junior high school science teacher. Sue decided that she wanted to spend more time with books than with numbers. She went back to college and took the required education courses. Due to the influence of an elementary science teacher, Sue decided to become a science teacher. Sue has been teaching science to seventh graders in a suburban junior high school for nine years.

Sue finds that science teachers do considerable reading. She usually has one concentrated preparation period each week. During this time, she will read for 3 to 4 hours. Besides reading the teacher's manual, she reads the actual students' book. Then she takes notes and makes outlines for herself and her students. Arriving an hour early every morning gives Sue the time to read over all her notes and outlines for the day along with reading and preparing for the laboratory work her students will be doing.

Sue's reading time is not just devoted to preparing for her classes. She makes all her own tests, so she has to spend more hours rereading all the material to develop these tests. If she gives an essay test, she has to spend additional hours reading the students' papers. Sue reads for another 2 to 3 hours every evening so that she will be able to enhance what her students are reading in their textbooks. A bookworm since her childhood when she always received a book for Christmas, Sue has found a career that lets her read.

Teaching at the High School Level

Giving students objectives before each reading assignment is Felice Knarr's way of developing critical readers in her twelfth-grade English literature classes. Felice has been teaching English at a private high school for nine years.

In August, before school starts, Felice charts out her course of study for the entire school year. She reads every book that the students will be reading so that she knows how long each reading assignment should take. This is not the only time Felice reads the material that will be assigned to her students. Before each reading assignment is made, she rereads the material to develop the objectives for her lesson plans. Beyond all the reading that Felice does in her preparation, she also spends 6 to 8 hours a week grading the essays and compositions of her 100 students. This does not include the reading that she must do in grading vocabulary, spelling, and short writing assignments.

Felice is a true bookworm who seems to always be reading. She spends several hours each day reading academic journals. It is not uncommon for her to spend 8 to 12 hours on weekends keeping up with her academic reading because she is taking courses to complete her master's degree in English. For relaxation, Felice likes to read magazines.

Teaching at the College Level

The usual entry teaching position at college is as an assistant professor. Then the battle commences to get tenure, which is permanent status as a faulty member. During the trial years before tenure is granted, which ranges from seven to ten years, assistant professors struggle valiantly to make names for themselves. The usual route to doing this at universities is by publishing papers for journals and books. This is the reason for the expression "publish or perish."

During this probationary period, reading fills every spare minute of assistant professors' time as research is done to produce the needed publications. The reading at this stage must necessarily be quite narrow within the teaching field. After the desired tenure is granted, reading can become much broader so that a fuller understanding of a field of study is achieved.

Assistant professors eventually become professors, and some even become department chairpersons. Reading is an absolute necessity throughout an academic career. Teachers at the college level must keep up with what is happening in their individual fields and must also read to develop new courses. Indeed, this career seems to be a perfect one for bookworms.

All Kinds of Teachers

There are many other teachers besides classroom teachers. Today, most elementary schools have reading teachers, speech teachers, music teachers, and physical education teachers on their teaching staffs. These teachers have specialized in a particular subject area just as teachers in junior and senior high schools do. There are also teachers who work in gifted and talented programs and in special education. Some teachers become counselors, curriculum directors, and principals

Other Positions in the Field of Education

Bookworms who are interested in education but don't want to work in the classroom can find satisfying jobs outside of the classroom that involve reading.

College Admissions Counselor

According to Steve Bushouse, former dean of admissions at Butler University in Indianapolis, you need strong basic reading skills to work as an admissions counselor at a college. However, he points out, you need to have other skills too in order to be successful at this job. People in the admissions office also need to be very people-oriented. Not only do admissions counselors interview students, they also give speeches at schools and work in booths at college fairs.

College admissions counselors read and evaluate high school records. Then as part of a committee they decide which students will be admitted to a college. In this job, entire days—far into the night—are spent reading. Furthermore, this is not a five-day-a-week job, especially when applications are being read. Quite frequently, this job is held by recent college graduates.

State Department of Education

The Department of Education in each state has advisory positions that would appeal to bookworms. One position that involves reading is working as a reading consultant. These consultants need to read widely so that they can advise teachers on the wide variety of materials that can be used in the classroom. Jobs in curriculum planning should also interest bookworms.

Education Associations and Organizations

In the United States, there are many professional organizations for teachers. The National Education Association (NEA) has the largest membership. The American Federation of Teachers (AFT) is a teaching union that works to improve teaching conditions. There are also professional associations like the National Association of Secondary School Principals. All of the education organizations and associations offer jobs for educators in different capacities from researching to copyediting.

Travel Opportunities for Teachers

If you are a bookworm who likes to travel, there are many teaching jobs in all parts of the world. The pay is not always as good as it is in the United States, but the opportunities for travel and adventure are often an added pull for bookworms looking for excitement. If you are interested in working abroad as a teacher, you may want to write to some of the organizations listed below:

USIA
Fullbright Teacher Exchange Program
E/ASX, Room 353
301 Fourth Street SW
Washington, DC 20547

Office of Overseas Schools
A/OS, Room 245, SA-29
Department of State
Washington, DC 20522-2902

Peace Corps Recruiting Office
1990 K Street NW
Washington, DC 20526

International Schools Services
P.O. Box 5910
Princeton, NJ 08543

U.S. Department of Defense
Dependents Schools
2461 Eisenhower Avenue
Alexandria, VA 22331-1100

Teachers' Salaries

Teachers' salaries are constantly increasing, although they vary
greatly among states. Can you guess which state has the highest
salary for teachers? Is it California, New York, Alaska, Pennsylvania, Hawaii, or Connecticut? If you picked Connecticut, you
are correct. In 1993, all teachers in Connecticut averaged
$48,300. Alaska was second with an average salary of $46,000. If
you are interested in knowing what the starting salaries for
schools in your area are, you can get this information from your
State Department of Education or your local school district. The
average starting salaries for all teachers was $22,505 in 1993.

Teachers' salaries usually increase each year based on merit,
years of experience, and educational degrees. In some states,

secondary schoolteachers receive higher pay than elementary schoolteachers. The average salary for college professors is approximately $46,000 a year for full-time faculty members on nine-month contracts.

For Further Reading

Teaching is a bookworm's career today more than ever. The responsibilities and workloads of teachers have increased along with the volume of reading that must be done in order to keep pace with the rapid accumulation of knowledge. The following books will give you a good look at what the teaching profession is like:

Dunham, Jack. *Stress in Teaching*. New York, N.Y.: Nicholas Publishing, 1992.
Edelfelt, Roy A. *Careers in Education*. Lincolnwood, Ill.: NTC Publishiug Group, 1993.
Fine, Janet. *Opportunities in Teaching Careers*. Lincolnwood, Ill.: NTC Publishing Group, 1994.
Krannich, Ronald R. *The Educator's Guide to Alternative Jobs & Careers*. Manassas, Va.: Impact Publications, 1991.
National Education Association. *Teaching Career Fact Book*. Washington, D.C. (annual).

CHAPTER SEVEN

Research Careers

Seeking and Assembling Information

W hat kind of material do you like to read? Is it history, astronomy, religion, or medical science? Perhaps you prefer space science, ecology, government relations, or education. No matter what you like to read, just as long as it's primarily nonfiction, there is probably a job somewhere in research that will let you read material that really interests you.

Research jobs involve seeking information so that papers and books can be written by university and research center scholars and historians. They also involve reading material so that it can be sorted into some kind of order as archivists do. Much research is also done for local, state, and federal governments; museums; and businesses.

More than any other country in the world, the United States has recognized the importance of research both in the public and private sector. Just the number of research organizations is mind-boggling. There are more than 11,700 university and nonprofit research organizations. Many of these organizations, however, have small staffs.

Research Jobs at Universities

Universities are true research centers. A large university has numerous research projects going on all the time. Jobs become available whenever a new project is started. Many university projects are headed by resident faculty members; others will be led by accomplished scholars from other universities who have come to the university to work on a research project. To head a project, you must have outstanding credentials. A doctorate degree is just a basic requirement. Then you have to demonstrate that you are an expert in your field.

Fortunately for those who want to be researchers at a university, research projects need to have more staff than the one person heading the project, who may only work at it part-time. Although people seeking research staff positions don't have to have the same professional status as the project heads, they do have to have top-notch qualifications to land these desirable jobs. The competition for jobs as entry-level research assistants can be so intense at prestigious universities that you could be competing against 50 or more applicants.

The Research Assistant Job

There are different levels of research assistants. To climb each rung on the ladder, or to start beyond an entry-level position, you will need more than a bachelor's degree, plus experience. You will also have to demonstrate that you have a working knowledge of scientific theory and can evaluate and analyze what you read. As you move to higher levels, your responsibilities will increase. You may become responsible for a phase of a project or for an entire project.

You can find out about entry-level jobs in research through university employment offices or bulletins. These jobs will not require as much reading as bookworms would probably like. Usually, you can expect to spend about half of your time extracting information from a library—that's the reading portion of the job—and the other half doing clerical work. In fact, having some clerical experience or at least knowing how to use a computer and file is almost a prerequisite for getting entry-level jobs.

As a research assistant, you usually only work on one project at a time for a scholar. This does give you the opportunity to become a miniexpert on a subject through your reading. Some projects have a time limit, while others go on as more funding becomes available. After one project is finished, you will typically go on to work on another project.

Research Jobs at Think Tanks

If you are constantly reading newspapers and news magazines to keep up with what is going on in the world and would like doing this for a living, then a job at a think tank could be ideal for you. Think tanks are strictly American. No other country has private institutions that are dedicated to public-policy research. The United States has more than 100 think tanks that are not associated with the government or colleges, or universities.

When you hear the words, "think tank," you may conjure up visions of intellectuals concentrating on heady problems. It is decidedly true that considerable thinking goes on at think tanks, but much of that thinking is based upon reading.

When the first think tanks emerged in the early decades of this century, research resulted in books and papers that influenced public decisions. Today's think tanks are more activist. While still producing books and papers (the Heritage Foundation produces more than 200 policy papers a year), think tanks also actively lobby legislators and court the press to influence the government. So besides researching and writing, the think tank employee's job description has to be rewritten to include public relations work.

The first generation of think tanks was slightly to the left or right of center in its political thinking. However, its research tended to show both viewpoints. A new generation of think tanks that had strong conservative roots emerged during the mid-1970s and is flourishing today. People thinking of applying for a job at a think tank should probably consider their own political biases when deciding where to look for a job. Note the political leanings of these prominent think tanks.

Conservative

American Enterprise Institute

Heritage Foundation

Hoover Institution

Hudson Institute

Manhattan Institute

Liberal

Center for Defense Information

Center for National Policy

Council on Economic Priorities

Institute for Policy Studies

World Policy Institute

If you want to work in North Dakota or Florida, you would have had trouble until recently finding a job with a think tank. There are now a few state-based think tanks concerned with state, not national, issues. Traditionally, most think tanks are located close to Washington, D.C. or New York City, although there are exceptions. One of the earliest conservative think tanks, the Hoover Institution, which was founded in 1919, is located in California. The Hudson Institute really overturned the East Coast location emphasis by moving from a location 45 miles from New York City to Indianapolis, Indiana, in 1984.

Working at a Think Tank

You may bump into people like Gerald Ford, Henry Kissinger, Mikhail Gorbachev, Zbigniew Brzezinski, or Dan Quayle if you work at a think tank. Many of the high-level jobs are held by people who have been in the public limelight. Of course, most of the people working at think tanks don't have names that you see every day in the newspaper. But many are quite well-known scholars in their field of expertise or show promise of being future academic superstars.

At the older think tanks, you are more likely to work with well-known scholars and people who have made their names in government. Charles Schultze, who was the chairman of the Council of Economic Advisers under Carter, is now at Brookings, while former UN Ambassador Jeane Kirkpatrick is at the American Enterprise Institute. The stars at the newer think tanks tend to be political activists instead of former government officials.

First-level Researcher

If your vision of the perfect job is one where your desk is inundated with reading materials, an entry-level job at a think tank may be the right one for you. To get this type of job, impressive credentials are needed. For most jobs, some type of graduate degree—usually a master's degree—is essential. You also should have some experience in doing research, even if it is only writing your own research papers. When seeking a job it can be helpful to know someone involved in a project at a think tank in order to discover what jobs are available; however, sending out résumés is also a good way to get a job.

If you have a job as a first-level researcher, you can work on researching just one topic for a think tank scholar or on a number of topics for different people. When a project starts up, you will read to get a basic understanding of an issue. Then you may be asked to develop a bibliography for the head of the project. At times you will summarize what you read. You may even be given a particular issue on which to focus. You will have considerable autonomy in deciding how your job will be performed. Ultimately, scholars at the think tank write papers or books on the topics that have been researched.

To advance up the ladder from a first-level researcher, a doctorate is usually required. To get a feel for what a job is like at a think tank, you should consider taking an internship at one of these institutions.

Archivists Are Researchers and Readers

Not too many people are acquainted with what archives are or what archivists do. First of all, archives are records of individuals, groups, institutions, and governments at all levels that are preserved because they have information of lasting value. Such historic documents as the Declaration of Independence, the U.S. Constitution, and the Bill of Rights are preserved in the National Archives Building in Washington, D.C. All the valuable documents from each president's term of office are preserved in presidential libraries, which are archives. You can also find the records that must be kept by law for local and state governments in archives. Archival records are not just government documents. Businesses have archives; so do universities, hospitals, labor unions, and even small historical societies.

Before the age of computers, microfilm, and recordings, archives were chiefly made up of unpublished manuscripts. Now archives contain records in such additional formats as computer tapes, photographs, films, and sound recordings.

The Job of an Archivist

The primary job of an archivist is to establish control over records. This involves organizing records so that they can easily be accessed. A collection must have a title, and all of the contents must be organized in a logical sequence and described so that they can be used. The job also requires a judgment of what records have historical value; for example, the federal government only saves 3 percent of its records. Much of the work of the archivist, therefore, is going through documents to decide which should be kept permanently. All of these tasks require reading. Not only must the documents be read, the archivist needs to have an understanding of the historical period in which they were created to understand their value.

Another job of the archivist is overseeing the preservation of documents. Because original newsprint will not last, the archivist must supervise the reproduction of newspaper clippings onto acid-free paper. Archivists must also determine whether to restore or conserve an original document by microfilming or some other technique or to both restore and reproduce the original. The preservation is done by scientific and technical specialists.

The archivist's job also includes gathering information that is requested. Archivists are becoming more involved, too, in the publication of materials and in their exhibition. In addition, some archivists have the task of soliciting funds to preserve or establish a collection. And, of course, archivists who are in charge of collections have administrative responsibilities involved in supervising a staff.

What you earn as an archivist varies with where you work. Generally, the larger or better-funded institutions offer larger salaries. Beginning archivists' salaries are comparable to those of teachers.

Requirements for Becoming an Archivist

After a person decides to be an archivist, it is usually a lifetime career. At first archivists may move from one archive to another, but most eventually stay in one place. And that place may well be a governmental unit because the majority of archivists have civil service standing. Those who work at universities may also be faculty members.

The one personal characteristic that archivists have in common, no matter where they work, is an interest in preserving the past. There is also a need for organizational ability, good judgment, an interest in research, and self-reliance.

While there may be some entry-level jobs that require only a bachelor's degree, a master's degree is much more common. Undergraduate majors can vary, but master's degrees are usually in either American history or library science. Increasingly, job candidates have master's degrees in both areas with coursework in the theory and practice of archives. Only two schools offer master's degree programs in archival studies. For senior staff positions, especially at universities, a doctoral degree may be required.

The archival profession is a growing one. One way to learn more about this profession is by contacting The Society of American Archivists (SAA), 600 South Federal, Suite 504, Chicago, Illinois 60605.

Curators Are Researchers and Readers

Like archivists, curators are concerned with keeping records of the past. The difference is that archivists are primarily concerned with written material and curators are primarily concerned with man-made objects and specimens. You will find curators at museums, zoos, aquariums, botanic gardens, and historic sites. Curators who work for the federal government are found at the Smithsonian Institution, military museums, and in archeological and other museums run by the Department of the Interior.

The Curator's Job

A curator's job will vary depending on the size of the place where the curator works. In a small institution, the curator must not only acquire, identify, catalog, and store objects but also restore objects, arrange for exhibitions, and conduct educational programs. This job description can be further expanded to include hammering and nailing and doing all the research when it comes to setting up an exhibition. At a large institution, a curator's job would be more specific. A curator might specialize in a particular area like toys, anthropology, science, or technology or be assigned a function like cataloging, acquisition, or restoring the collection.

Whether a curator has a specific responsibility or is responsible for everything at an institution, considerable reading is essential in this job. When an institution acquires new objects or specimens, curators must read to identify them accurately. When a new exhibit is being set up, the curator researches to see what belongs in the exhibit and that everything is properly displayed. Curators must also read to find out about the newest and best ways to preserve and display objects and specimens. There is also reading to answer questions posed by the public. And of course considerable reading of professional journals is essential to keep up with what is happening in the profession.

Requirements for Becoming a Curator

While some curators have bachelor's or master's degrees in museum studies (museology), many institutions are looking for curators with degrees in specific areas like art, anthropology, biology, or history. The minimum requirements for obtaining a curator's job are a bachelor's degree and experience. Most museums, however, want curators to have a master's degree in a specific field plus experience. Curators working in smaller institutions may also need some business courses to handle administrative responsibilities.

Fewer than 10,000 jobs are available for archivists and curators. Because of the current interest in art, history, technology, and culture, the number of curators is growing. However, there will never be a great number of openings for jobs as curators. Furthermore, the job is appealing to many qualified applicants, so there is considerable competition. Those who have had experience as interns or volunteers often have the best chance to get these coveted jobs. The pay for beginning archivists and curators usually starts in the low 20s. Pay will generally be higher at large well-funded museums and government jobs than at smaller organizations or museums. Curators' salaries are similar to those of archivists.

Historians Read about the Past

Why did Winston Churchill lose his post as prime minister after successfully leading Britain through World War II? How successful was the first Five-Year Plan in China in terms of stimulating agricultural production? Historians formulate questions like these to direct their study of the past. They are imaginative researchers who read all kinds of documents to determine what happened in the past, why it happened, and how it has affected the present and may affect the future. After collecting data by reading vast amounts of material, historians analyze it and then present it in the form of textbooks, lectures, studies, reports, and articles.

Most historians, more than 70 percent of them, are college teachers who research and write as well as carry out their teaching duties. The remaining historians work at jobs where their historical skills and knowledge are required. This may mean writing histories for companies and governmental units. It can mean researching historical records for businesses, law firms, television or movie companies, and public agencies. It can also mean analyzing past trends for banks, insurance companies, investment services, manufacturers, utilities, and public relations firms. No matter where a historian works, the job is ideal for bookworms because it always allows them to bury their noses in books and read while they are doing their jobs.

Education and Job Opportunities

Because most historians work as college teachers, a doctorate in history is almost essential to obtain employment. Teaching jobs open up when faculty members retire or enrollment in history courses increases.

Opportunity to obtain a position as a historian is very limited. Overall, less than 1,000 job openings for historians occur each year. There is keen competition for these openings whether they are at colleges, museums, archives, historical societies, businesses, or with the government. Only a few historians are self-employed as writers, consultants, or researchers.

A Historian in Women's Studies

Until a few years ago, the role of women was overlooked in history. There was a dearth of material written on this subject. Sara Evans, a University of Minnesota professor, is a historian who recognized that the history of women was undervalued. Hired by the university to teach women's history, Sara combined this job with the writing of scholarly works on women. Her approach is not to romanticize the role of women by telling of heroines but to prove that women whose names aren't household words have helped to shape the United States.

Sara's research has taken her to libraries, museums, and archives to answer questions about the past. An important part of her research has been figuring out what type of material to study. For example, to find out about the diet and workload of slaves, her students have studied plantation records.

Both Sara's teaching duties and research in women's studies have entailed considerable reading. Obviously, historians are readers; however, the time Sara spends reading varies enormously. When she is on leave, she will read as much as 40 hours a week. The pluses to her work are that she feels she is doing something new all the time and that her work is making a difference in the way people see the past.

Researchers for Publishers

When you read an article in an encyclopedia, the *New Yorker*, *National Geographic*, *Newsweek*, or *Time*, you expect the facts to be accurate. There is a small brigade of workers at these organizations who research to make sure that what you read is accurate. They are seekers of the truth, whether their job titles are fact checkers, junior researchers, or senior researchers. These researchers spend their days reading and phoning as they go over articles word-by-word to make them reliable. The backgrounds of these researchers vary. However, a knowledge of research techniques and an insatiable desire to find the true facts are essential. It is also necessary to be able to write clearly because these researchers must write about changes and explain proposed changes.

Researching for an Encyclopedia

As a child, Cheryl Graham would read *Nancy Drew* books and dream of being a detective. Today, as a senior researcher for World Book Publishing, she fulfills that dream as she acts as a sleuth digging up hard-to-find facts for the encyclopedia and other publications. Being a fact detective involves using the computer to retrieve wire services and newspapers, and looking up information in printed sources. Four months of the year, Cheryl spends her time updating the World Book Encyclopedia, which must include recent happenings. The rest of the year Cheryl is primarily concerned with checking the facts of articles submitted by contributors. It may take her a day to check the facts on an article about Jim Henson, creator of the Muppets. However, an article on environmental pollution could require as long as a month to check the facts thoroughly because it involves talking with experts and finding many different sources.

All of Cheryl's jobs have involved considerable reading. At her first job with the Library of Congress, she set up a library for congressional researchers doing research on environmental policy. This meant sitting down and reading articles like crazy so she could abstract and index them. She then worked at two other libraries as a reference librarian before coming to World Book 14 years ago. This bookworm never tires of looking up interesting facts and reading about them.

Information Brokers

When businesses or organizations need specific information to solve problems or answer questions, they call in information brokers. Being an information broker is essentially being a researcher. It is also being a reader because brokers use libraries and on-line databases to find specific information for their clients. Some brokers specialize in a particular area, such as the environment, biotech, or patents. Careers in information brokering have really just emerged in the past 25 years. Choose a career in this area and you will probably work alone; there are few information-brokering companies. And each job will bring a new challenge to find information, so you will never be bored. To be a successful information broker, you will need solid research skills, computer expertise, and the ability to market yourself.

For Further Reading

So much of research involves reading. Here is a job that truly allows bookworms to combine avocation with vocation. The following books will give you more information on careers in research:

Barzun, Jacques and Henry F. Graff. *The Modern Researcher*. 5th edition. Orlando, Fla.: Houghton Mifflin, 1992.

Ross, BevAnne. *Freelance: Research for Pay*. Novato, Calif.: Bar Publications, 1992.

Rugge, Sue and Alfred Glossbrenner. *The Information Broker's Handbook*. Oakland, Calif.: The Information Professionals Institute, 1995.

Smith, James A. *The Idea Brokers: Think Tanks and the Rise of the New Policy Elite*. New York, N.Y.: Macmillan, 1991.

CHAPTER EIGHT

Public Sector Careers
Reading for the Government

There is no shortage of jobs in the public sector. In fact, the government is the single largest employer in the United States. If you add the jobs of all the federal, state, and local governmental units together, you will find more than 16 million jobs in executive branch agencies. Add in all the positions at all levels for the legislative and judicial branches plus the Armed Forces, and the total number of government jobs approaches 18 million. Within this great number of jobs, many will appeal to bookworms. Some are identical to jobs in the private sector, while others are unique to the public sector.

Jobs in the public sector offer certain advantages. First of all, there is usually more long-term job security than in the private sector. Most jobs will pay salaries comparable to those earned in the private sector. The benefits, however, may be more generous in the public sector, especially vacation and sick leave benefits. In addition, employees can count on annual raises.

Working for the Federal Government

More than 3 million civilian employees work for agencies of the executive branch of the federal government. They work in more than 900 different occupations for more than 100 different agencies. They don't just work in Washington, D.C. In fact, close to 80 percent work in other geographical areas including the 6 percent who work abroad. What's more, you can often keep the same job and move from state to state or even city to city.

Sixty percent of the federal workers are involved in just two jobs: delivering the mail and providing for the national defense. The rest of the workers are almost evenly divided among these activities: management of natural resources and transportation, administration of benefit payments to states and assistance to states and localities, provision of health care to war veterans, tax collection and other general government management, and research and information activities. It is within this last category that most bookworms will find their job niche in the government.

Although people tend to think that the number of people working for the federal government is growing rapidly, this is certainly not true. The period of rapid growth was the 1960s and 1970s. In the past decade, federal employment grew by about 7 percent, while nonfederal employment expanded approximately 25 percent. Still, many jobs are available, especially as replacements. Frequently, as many as 20,000 people are hired by the federal government in a month.

How to Find Out about Jobs

Perhaps one of the hardest things to do is to find out where the jobs in government are that would appeal to you as a bookworm. In general, the category where you will find these jobs is the GS-100 group, which is social science, psychology, and welfare; and the GS-1000 group, which is information and arts. You can learn more about these jobs by reading *The Guide to Federal Jobs*, which provides job descriptions.

After you have an idea of what kind of job you are looking for, you have the difficult task of finding out where vacancies for those jobs exist. The federal government is quite decentralized, so you can't just go to one spot and find out about all the jobs that are available. Some job vacancies are advertised in newspapers. You can also find listings in professional journals. A college placement office is another place to find out about positions. In addition, state employment offices will have lists of job vacancies. You can also visit, write, or phone federal job information centers. The federal government has divided the country into ten regions, and you will find at least one job information center in each region. One of the best places to find job information is at a regional office of a government agency because agencies must post all their vacancies. You can find the addresses and phone numbers of job information centers and regional offices of government agencies at a public library.

Although the federal government does not publish a complete list of all job openings, several private companies publish lists of jobs currently available. You should be able to find this information in *Federal Career Opportunities* and *Federal Jobs Digest*, which are available in public libraries.

How to Get a Job

Whenever you find out about a job opening, you should get a copy of the vacancy announcement. It will give you all the details that you must have to apply successfully for the job. It provides the exact identifying number of the job, which you must have because the same job could be found in more than one agency. It will give the deadlines for submitting an application. It also provides helpful information on salary, job title, number of positions available, the location of the job, the description of the job, and the qualifications required for the job. This announcement can be obtained from the agency that has the vacancy.

To apply for most jobs in the federal government you have to complete an application form—formally called Standard Form 171 or more usually known as SF-171. This is your résumé, and it will play a large role in determining whether you will even get an interview for a position. Rather than just completing this application once, it should be revised to suit each job you apply for. This is because applications are evaluated for each job on the basis of the job's duties and your qualifications. Besides formally submitting an application for a job, it is also helpful to contact individuals who hire at agencies that interest you for advice, information, and possible interviews.

Jobs That Pay You to Read

Jobs that involve doing studies and research—and there are many in these categories within the federal government—are the ones that are literally going to pay you to read. One such job is as a social science analyst. There are approximately 15,000 jobs in this category located in different government units throughout the country. Because this position is very desirable, the competition for entry-level positions is keen. Many job seekers will have master's degrees when only a bachelor's degree is required.

Another area in which bookworms may find jobs is within the intelligence community. This includes the Central Intelligence Agency, the Federal Bureau of Investigation, the Drug Enforcement Agency, and other related agencies. The National Archives, presidential libraries, the Smithsonian Institution, and the National Trust for Historic Preservation are additional places where bookworms should look for jobs.

Jobs in the Legislative and Judicial Branches

Although the lion's share of jobs in the federal government is found in agencies of the executive branch, jobs in the legislative and judicial branches are also available. You can find out about these jobs in some of the same ways that you find out about jobs in the executive branch. However, you will have to contact each legislative agency to find out about specific job vacancies and hiring procedures. Many of the agencies will have job hotline numbers. On the legislative side, bookworms are most likely to find appealing jobs at the General Accounting office, the Library of Congress, the Government Printing office, and the Congressional Budget office.

Jobs at the Library of Congress

An excellent place for bookworms to find jobs is in the Congressional Research Service of the Library of Congress. Hundreds of social science analysts are employed here to give members of Congress and congressional committees information and to make impartial analyses of pending policy issues. Analysts might be assigned to find out what the alternatives are to the current structure of congressional committees or the ways in which affordable housing can best be provided. The analysts will do research, compile materials, and gather the pros and cons on an issue. A senior researcher may put together his or her own data. Entire days can be spent doing nothing but on-the-job reading.

Jobs on Capitol Hill

Senators and representatives have offices both in Washington, D.C. and in their home districts. The Washington, D.C. staffs are larger and are better job bets for bookworms because they have staff members who will do some research. If you want a job with a senator or representative, it doesn't hurt to go to the congressperson's office. There is an unbelievable amount of competition for staff vacancies, and it can be helpful to have made contact with those who are doing the hiring.

Bookworms can also find jobs on legislative committees and subcommittees that require people who are experts in certain policy areas. Both the House and Senate have referral services where you can fill out applications that will be circulated to congressional offices, committees, and subcommittees. Their addresses and phone numbers are:

House Placement Office
The Ford House Office Building, Room 219
Washington, D.C. 20515
(202) 226-6732

Senate Placement Office
Hart Senate office Building, Room 142
Washington, D.C. 20510
(202)224-9167

Working for State Governments

There are actually more jobs at the state level than at the federal level. Many of these jobs are in higher education and libraries, which are favorite places for bookworms to work. Jobs at the state level in the executive, legislative, and judicial branches are similar to those in the federal government except that they obviously do not deal with international relations, nor do they usually pay as well.

You will find announcements of jobs in state government in many of the same ways that you find announcements of federal jobs. In addition, you will find job announcements in such places as bulletin boards in government buildings, public libraries, and community organizations. After you have found the announcement of a job that appeals to you, follow the instructions on the announcement to submit your application. It is also a good idea to contact people at agencies who are doing the hiring for job information.

Some Jobs for Bookworms

Look for jobs for social science analysts because these jobs will require considerable reading on the state level just as they do on the federal level. In most states, you will find some of these jobs in legislative auditor's offices. As an analyst, you would determine how well state programs like welfare or highway maintenance are working. Then reports would be written to give this information to the legislature. Job requirements for this position usually are a master's degree in an area like public affairs, economics, political science, or one of the social sciences plus some research experience. You can sometimes get a temporary position on a project that will lead to full-time employment.

Another state job that requires reading is the job of legislative analyst for a house or senate research department. These analysts draft bills and amendments, summarize bills, and do research studies. They are trying to apply academic research to public policy. Holders of these jobs have master's degrees or are lawyers. Knowing how to use a computer is essential.

Working for Local Governments

The largest number of people are employed in local governments—the cities, towns, counties, townships, and school districts. It is at this level that you can work closest to the people. The greatest number of employees in this group are teachers. Finding and getting a job at this level is often a very informal process especially in very small governmental units. Larger units will have personnel departments that have vacancy announcements.

Working as an Elected Official

Some elected officials find themselves absolutely drowning in materials to be read. Most legislators, at all government levels, can never get all their job-related reading done. The president, governors, and mayors of large cities all have so much reading to do that they frequently ask assistants to limit reports to one-page summaries. Judges also must necessarily spend much of their time reading.

For Further Reading

Because the federal government has so many jobs and hiring practices vary so much, bookworms who want to find jobs that let them read are going to have to do a lot of reading to find those jobs. It is absolutely essential to have an understanding of how the government works. In addition, you need to read books like the following ones that explain about the government and governmental jobs:

Baxter, Neale. *Opportunities in Federal Government Careers.* Lincolnwood, Ill.: NTC Publishing Group, 1992.

————. *Opportunities in State and Local Government.* Lincolnwood, Ill.: NTC Publishing Group, 1993.

Damp, Dennis. *The Book of U.S. Government Jobs.* Coraopolis, Pa.: D-Amp Publications, 1991.

Goldenkoff, Robert and Dana Morgan. *Federal Jobs for College Graduates.* New York, N.Y.: Prentice Hall, 1991.

Krannich, Ronald L. and Caryl Rae Krannich. *Find a Federal Job Fast! Cutting the Red Tape of Getting Hired.* Manassas, Va.: Impact Publications, 1991.

Krannich, Ronald. *Right SF-170 Writer: The Complete Guide to Communicating Your Qualifications to Federal Employers*. Manassas, Va.: Impact Publications, 1992.

Lauber, Daniel. *Government Job Finder*. River Forest, Ill.: Planning Communications, 1994.

Rutsohn, Rita G. , ed. *America's Federal Jobs*. Indianapolis, Ind.: JIST Works, Inc., 1991.

Working for Your Uncle: The Complete Guide to Finding a Job with the Federal Government. Ossining, N.Y.: Breakthrough Publications, 1993.

CHAPTER NINE

Private Sector Careers
Reading for the Profit Makers

Although the government is the largest single employer in the United States, approximately nine out of ten people work in the private sector. Obviously, this is where bookworms will find most of the jobs that involve reading. You have already read about the jobs in publishing, glamour industries, and research in this sector. Now you will find out about all the professional and business jobs that should be filled by people who love to read.

With the constant explosion of new technology and knowledge in almost every field, few employees can afford not to read to keep up with what is happening in their area of employment. The secret is to find the jobs that require more than routine reading. Quite often these jobs will be found in areas where research is done.

If a bookworm has a specific field of interest, it may be possible to turn this interest into a job asset. The reader who has developed an in-depth knowledge of an industry, a country, or a product is a more attractive candidate for a job than someone who will have to learn vital background information on the job.

Reading Jobs in Traditional Professions

Occupations that require advanced education and training and also involve intellectual skills, such as medicine, law, engineering, theology, and teaching are regarded as professions. If you

111

have an intense interest in one of these professions, it is possible to find a job within it that lets you read. First of all, you can become a teacher of future doctors, lawyers, engineers, teachers, or other professionals at a college. Second, you can look for a job in the profession that emphasizes research. Third, because many professions allow one to be self-employed, you can tailor your job to fit your love of reading.

Doctors Read

Doctors who teach and those who work at research institutions spend much of their time reading—not only to increase their understanding but also in order to write papers. Even a doctor who primarily treats patients will find it essential to do at least 4 or 5 hours a week of solid professional reading beyond the routine reading of charts.

Lawyers Read

The younger lawyers are, the more they read because they need to do more research. It is not unusual for a junior attorney in a law firm to spend 3 or 4 hours a day reading briefs and cases. In addition, law clerks for judges, especially appellate judges, do a lot of reading. As lawyers become more senior, their reading time decreases. Still, most will be reading from 1½ to 2 hours a day, and it is not unusual for them to read 3 hours. Nowadays, more and more of this reading is done on computers rather than in law books because information can be accessed faster in this way.

Lawyers do not just practice law. One job that requires a legal background as well as very intense reading is putting head notes on cases for publishers of law books. Another job is as teacher in a law school.

Engineers Read

A career as an engineer could be in any one of 25 major specialties, which are further divided into numerous subdivisions. Engineers must read to keep abreast of the latest scientific dis-

coveries in their field because engineers are often the link between scientific discoveries and their applications. They must
learn about such things as the development of new and improved
materials in order to design and build machinery, roads, bridges,
power plants, cars, factories, and products. While their reading is
concentrated on technical journals, they must also read to learn
about governmental regulations affecting their work, especially
in the area of environmental concerns.

Members of the Clergy Read

Reading for members of the clergy can be for contemplation,
getting information for sermons, learning more about one's faith,
and increasing knowledge in an area like counseling.

The Money-People Read

When people buy stocks and bonds (securities), they usually deal
with stockbrokers. Because things are always changing so fast in
these markets, brokers have to snatch every moment they can to
keep up with what is happening. Unfortunately, not too much of
this time can take place during the day when the market is open
and they are busy dealing with clients. Also, because they receive
absolutely reams of material to digest, much of their reading must
just be skimming.

If you are fascinated by what is happening in the securities
market, there are research jobs in the investment area that are
made just for bookworms. On the sell side, the jobs are with
brokerage firms and investment banks that sell securities to
investors; while on the buy side, the jobs are with bank trust
departments, insurance companies, and fund management firms.

On the sell side, researchers look at securities to determine the
most attractive investments for their firm's clients. On the buy
side, researchers spend their time figuring out what should be
bought and sold for their firm's portfolio. On either side,
knowledge increases the probability that a decision will be a
correct one. Researchers read constantly to stay up-to-date with

what is happening because things change every day. Stocks and bonds that appear to be an excellent investment at the start of a week may be a poor choice by the end of the week.

Most researchers are assigned a specific industry. Within that area they will read all the information that they can get their hands on about the industry, firms in the industry, related government regulations, and world events that will affect the industry. Weather, revolutions, and governmental policy changes are just a few of the things that can change the value of securities. Besides reading, much time is spent talking to people to find out what is happening. After information is gathered, reports must be written to share that information.

If you decide to work as a researcher in the securities industry, you are likely to be working in New York City, which is the financial headquarters for more firms than any other place. It is important for you to know that employment in these firms is very cyclical. When times are good, employment is up. After contractions in the market, the number of employees is quickly reduced.

There is a very high level of competition for positions as researchers in the securities industry. It is possible for recent college graduates to enter this field and learn on the job. However, senior researchers will usually have master's degrees in business. More and more also have attained the professional designation chartered financial analyst (CFA), which is obtained after passing a series of three tests and showing experience in the field.

Bank Economists Read

The management team at a bank needs to know what is happening around the world in the economy. At banks that have $10 billion or more in deposits, there are economists. The chief economist is likely to have a doctorate in economics. Assistants will probably also have advanced degrees. However, there are entry-level jobs for college graduates with majors in economics. At all levels, reading is done so reports can be written on the economy for the bank and its clients.

Information Services Need Readers

Among the fastest-growing businesses in the economy are the information services companies that generate, process, and distribute data. With the world just about drowning in information, businesses, schools, professional people, the government, and even students researching papers need help to quickly find information. And this demand for information will just accelerate with the implementation of the Information Superhighway and further increase the use of information services.

Information services professionals get paid to read about the arts, environment, photography, and many other topics. Many work as indexers and abstractors for information services companies, where they read journals, magazines, and newspapers, organize bibliographic information, and write abstracts for articles. Writing an abstract involves reflecting the author's opinion. Many companies have a training period for this job when employees learn editorial policy, what goes into abstracts, how to organize and select material, and what plagiarism is. Of course, you have to love to read to enjoy this job. Other job requirements usually include a college degree, expertise in grammar, computer literacy, and an ability to record information accurately.

At some information services companies, you must work on-site. Others let you work at home and send your work in by modem. Although there are deadlines, you are often free to structure when you work. This flexibility makes the job appealing to many people, and the nature of the work itself is perfectly suited to bookworms.

Information Givers Are Readers

With the explosion of information, it is becoming more and more difficult for people in the public and private sectors to keep on top of everything that they should know in order to do their jobs effectively. For that reason, there are firms designed to just provide information. Usually, this information will be given in the form of reports, newsletters, speeches, and seminars. The people who supply this information must spend much of their time reading, sorting, and analyzing information. It is another excellent job for bookworms.

A Political Analyst

Julie Sedky reads from 40 to 50 percent of the time on her job as a political analyst at a firm that does public policy research for institutional investors. She tries to anticipate and analyze changes in governmental policy that will affect her clients, who invest other people's money and don't want to be surprised by what happens in Washington, D.C. She regularly reads such material as the *Washington Post, Wall Street Journal, Bureau of National Affairs Daily Report*, the *Congressional Quarterly*, the *Economist*, as well as excerpts from the *Congressional Record*, materials put out by the Congressional Budget Office and congressional leaders, and a number of private newsletters that tell what's going on in Washington, D.C. Julie's expertise in finding information is such that she sometimes finds her own words in references.

Consultants Are Readers

Consultants act as problem solvers in both the public and private sectors. They are also hired to do work similar to that done in think tanks. Being a consultant means doing research and analysis for a client. It could involve determining how a scarcity of labor would affect a firm. It might be a question of determining what the major trends in an industry are. No matter what the task, the major tool for accomplishing it is always reading.

While consulting firms vary in size from one-person operations to large international corporations, it is at the larger firms that most entry-level positions are found. Recent college graduates can get jobs as assistants on projects. You can find out the names of consulting firms by looking at the *National Directory of Consulting Firms*.

Corporate America Needs Readers

The companies that make soap, frozen dinners, paper, and automobiles, as well as the companies that drill for oil or build airplanes, have jobs for bookworms. No matter what a company produces—if it is large enough—there will be jobs that require reading. When you look for a job in corporate America, be sure to investigate areas like human resources, consumer relations, and marketing research.

Human Resources Departments Deal with People

All the hiring and firing of employees, the negotiating of labor agreements, and the determining of benefits and salaries are done in the human resources department at a large company. This is the department that deals with all the people who work at a company. Because the federal government as well as state governments have many laws that spell out exactly how employees are to be treated, employees in this department must do a lot of reading just to keep up with statutory requirements. Then they have to make sure that the people in operations know what these laws are and follow them.

Terri Nelson works for a Fortune 500 food company as a placement specialist. This is not a job that you can just step into because so many companies want college graduates who have experience, and there are few training positions. Many placement specialists begin as clerical workers to get basic business experience. Terri, who has a college degree, worked as a secretary in human resources, a bookkeeper, and a customer service representative before becoming a placement specialist.

During a typical week, Terri may read as many as 500 résumés of people seeking employment with her company. She is looking for people who meet the qualifications for positions that are available. She will review the résumés of all the qualified candidates for a position and then write down questions to ask each of these applicants. Besides reading résumés, she also interviews applicants and conducts an orientation program for new employees.

Terri estimates that she reads 70 to 80 percent of the time on the job. Besides reading résumés, she keeps up with the literature in her field and reads government rulings.

Consumer Relations Departments Deal with Customers

When consumers are unhappy, they write to companies to voice their complaints. Companies receive mail asking why a prize was not included in a cereal box as promised or complaining that a new car has needed numerous adjustments. Companies also receive mail asking for information about such things as products or company activities. Letters may ask why a product isn't biodegradable or why a company is doing business with a certain country.

To keep their customer's goodwill, these letters are answered by employees in customer relations departments. Some employees read and answer mail all day, while others alternate between handling mail and telephone calls. Many letters can be answered by form letters that are personalized. Answering some letters requires research. Companies try to answer every letter as accurately as possible.

To get a job answering mail or the telephone, it is not always necessary to have a college degree. Employees do have to demonstrate an ability to write. In addition, here is a job where experience is not required.

Marketing Research

Some companies use information services to find out about marketing trends or how consumers like a product. Other companies have their own marketing research departments and may also use information services. Jobs in marketing research involve keeping in touch with what consumers want through test marketing and product testing. This includes the collection of data through research and reading. The background needed for this job varies from company to company. Many market researchers have a bachelor's degree in business and an advanced degree in marketing, finance, or accounting.

For Further Reading

Because the private sector is where most of the jobs are, this is the area where bookworms should do the most reading. Investigate what careers in different professions offer as well as what jobs with financial institutions and information services are like. Finally, read to find out about what jobs are available in corporate America. Reading the following books is just a starting point for learning about jobs in the private sector:

America's Top 300 Jobs. Indianapolis, Ind.: JIST Works, Inc., 1994.

Cohen, William A. *The Student's Guide to Finding a Superior Job*. San Diego, Calif.: Pfeiffer & Co., 1993.

Daniels, Peggy Kneffel and Susan E. Edgar, eds. *Job Seekers Guide to Private and Public Companies*. Detroit, Mich.: Gale Research Inc., 1994.

Graham, Lawrence Otis. *The Best Companies for Minorities*. New York, N.Y.: Penguin Group, 1993.

Krannich, Ronald L. and Caryl Rae. *The Best Jobs for the 1990s and into the 21st Century*. Manassas, Va.: Impact Publications, 1993.

Krannich, Ronald L. *Careering & Re-Careering for the 1990s*. Manassas, Va.: Impact Publications, 1993.

Stair, Lila B. and Dorothy Domkowski. *Careers in Business*. Lincolnwood, Ill.: NTC Publishing Group, 1992.

Wicks, Wendy and Ann Marie Cunningham. *Guide to Careers in Abstracting and Indexing*. Philadelphia, Pa.: National Federation of Abstracting & Information Services, 1992.

CHAPTER TEN

More Careers for Bookworms

Endless Opportunities

Some people are obsessed with sports; others are addicted to watching television. But true happiness for a bookworm is being paid to read. The purpose of this book is to give bookworms career ideas so that they can realize their dream of reading from 9 to 5. There are still more careers than have been mentioned in this book that are good choices for bookworms. You have to be creative to find some of them. Try browsing through an occupational handbook while thinking of your fondness for reading, and you will discover some of them. You can further expand your list of jobs that require reading by looking at want ads, visiting placement offices in schools, looking at job listings at state and federal employment information offices, and visiting private employment agencies. Furthermore, here are a few other careers that would be quite satisfying to bookworms.

Translator

A good translator needs to be able to change the written or printed word from one language to another. In order to do this, a translator really needs to be a bookworm in two languages. Translators are especially in demand in businesses, government agencies, and research organizations. Many also work for translation services or free-lance. This is a job that offers both full-time and part-time employment. Bookworms in this field need to be prepared to read all kinds of scientific, technical, commercial, and legal material.

Braille Transcriber

You will not get rich being a braille transcriber, but you will be providing a very important service to blind people who read braille. Braille transcribers turn the printed word on all kinds of subjects into braille. This can be done by using the function keys on a computer or by using a device called a braillewriter. To become proficient in these techniques could take almost two years. Braille transcribing also can be done by just typing exact copy and using special computer programs. The drawbacks to the computer programs are that they can't handle music and mathematics nor can they convey certain formats easily. You can find jobs as a braille transcriber within some school districts and at braille book publishers.

Books-on-Tape Reader

If you have an excellent reading voice, you may be able to find a job that pays you for reading aloud. As you have probably noticed, more and more books are now available on audiocassettes. People who make these recordings can earn hundreds of dollars a day. The problem is that obtaining one of these jobs is extremely difficult. Many of these readers are professional actors and broadcasters. Furthermore, recording studios are generally located only in metropolitan areas.

Recorder for the Blind

Although you will not get paid to make recordings for the blind, it can be a very satisfying activity for bookworms of all ages.

Several organizations can give you information about making these recordings. One organization is Recording for the Blind, which will send you a packet of information for volunteer readers if you write to: Recording for the Blind, 20 Roszel Road, Princeton, NJ 08540. The only thing that you need to do is to pass the vocal test; then you are ready to read in one of their 31 studios. Volunteers are required to read at least 2 hours a week and can usually read what interests them. For example, a person with a doctorate in computer science will not be reading a fifth-grade reader. And it does take a special volunteer to read a high school or college chemistry book so that blind students can understand the illustrations.

Genealogist

People want to know where their great-grandmother was born and what their great-great-grandfather did for a living. Genealogists help people learn about their ancestors. They research for clues in libraries, church records, courthouses, old letters, diaries, newspaper clippings, census records, and government archives. This job requires the keeping of careful records. It also requires people who like to work alone; most genealogists are self-employed. There are no formal educational requirements for becoming a genealogist. Although there are some courses in genealogy that can be helpful, most people acquire their job knowledge through other genealogists and reading material on genealogy.

Abstractor

If you enjoy independent research and doing very exacting work, you might like to be an abstractor for an abstract or title insurance company. This work involves finding all the records on a piece of property so a clear title can be issued when it is sold. Abstractors search through dusty volumes in the basements of courthouses and also use computers to find this information. They never stop reading all day long. Although you don't have to have a college education to be an abstractor, some courses in law, real estate, and business can be helpful. It takes from four to six years of on-the-job training to learn how to do all kinds of abstracts. Most abstractors work in metropolitan areas where there are usually job openings for this position.

Word Processor

Word processing can just be transcribing work and putting it into an attractive format. Or it can involve editing and revising letters, reports, and other printed materials. Although it is a job that involves considerable reading, it is essentially clerical in nature. One advantage of this job is the possibility of doing it from your home as a telecommuter.

Judge

Television has brought judges and their work into your home. Outside of the courtroom, judges must spend considerable time reading documents on pleadings and motions. They also have to research legal issues. The amount of reading judges do varies by their jurisdiction. General trial judges will not do as much reading as federal and state appellate court judges, who study lower court decisions to see if they should be upheld or overturned.

Wire Editor

If you are curious about what is happening in Australia, South Dakota, and every corner of the world, the job of editor for a news agency that distributes news and photographs to newspapers, radio and television stations, and news magazines is a good job for you. These editors sit in front of a computer screen and read news. They pull copy and edit it and also route copy to clients. It is a job that lets one read for almost 8 hours and also puts the news of the world at your fingertips.

Author

Without authors, there would not be books, magazines, textbooks, newsletters, pamphlets, bulletins, or newspapers for bookworms to read. Authors aren't just writers; many are bookworms, too. Think of all the research that has to be done by authors. Imagine how much reading James Michener had to do in order to write *Hawaii* or *Centennial*. Consider how much reading was done to write this book. And don't forget the tremendous amount of reading that authors of textbooks do. Indeed, being an author is a superb career for bookworms and other literary types.

Still More Careers

The more you think about the different kinds of material that people read, the longer your list of careers for bookworms will become. There are people who make crossword puzzles and people who make all kinds of tests, from achievement tests to intelligence tests. Then there are people who clip what others have written for clipping services.

The Future for Bookworms

The future is bright for bookworms seeking jobs that allow them to be paid for reading. Today's best jobs are in areas that require education, and as a group bookworms tend to be well educated. Bookworms will find even more jobs in the future in banking, education, law, research, and management consulting. And they will find a bonanza of reading jobs within the rapidly growing information services industry. As far as the public sector goes, most of the growth in government jobs will be at the state and local levels.

Because the number of jobs that require reading is closely tied to the amount of written material, the years ahead should offer bookworms more and more opportunities to combine avocation and vocation because the world is deluged with an ever-increasing volume of written information. It does look like bookworms can look forward to having their best companions, books, with them on their jobs in a great variety of careers.

VGM CAREER BOOKS

CAREER DIRECTORIES
Careers Encyclopedia
Dictionary of Occupational Titles
Occupational Outlook Handbook

CAREERS FOR
Animal Lovers
Bookworms
Caring People
Computer Buffs
Crafty People
Culture Lovers
Environmental Types
Fashion Plates
Film Buffs
Foreign Language Aficionados
Good Samaritans
Gourmets
Health Nuts
History Buffs
Kids at Heart
Nature Lovers
Night Owls
Number Crunchers
Plant Lovers
Shutterbugs
Sports Nuts
Travel Buffs
Writers

CAREERS IN
Accounting; Advertising; Business;
Child Care; Communications;
Computers; Education;
Engineering;
the Environment; Finance;
Government; Health Care; High
Tech; International Business;
Journalism; Law; Marketing;
Medicine; Science; Social &
Rehabilitation Services

CAREER PLANNING
Beating Job Burnout
Beginning Entrepreneur
Career Planning & Development for
College Students &
Recent Graduates
Career Change
Careers Checklists
College and Career Success for
Students with Learning Disabilities
Complete Guide to Career Etiquette
Cover Letters They Don't Forget
Dr. Job's Complete Career Guide
Executive Job Search Strategies

Guide to Basic Cover Letter
Writing
Guide to Basic Résumé Writing
Guide to Internet Job Searching
Guide to Temporary Employment
Job Interviewing for College
Students
Joyce Lain Kennedy's Career Book
Out of Uniform
Slam Dunk Résumés
The Parent's Crash Course in
Career Planning: Helping Your
College Student Succeed

CAREER PORTRAITS
Animals; Cars; Computers;
Electronics; Fashion;
Firefighting; Music; Nursing;
Sports; Teaching; Travel; Writing

GREAT JOBS FOR
Business Majors
Communications Majors
Engineering Majors
English Majors
Foreign Language Majors
History Majors
Psychology Majors

HOW TO
Apply to American Colleges and
Universities
Approach an Advertising Agency and
Walk Away with the Job You Want
Be a Super Sitter
Bounce Back Quickly After
Losing Your Job
Change Your Career
Choose the Right Career
Cómo escribir un currículum vitae
en inglés que tenga éxito
Find Your New Career Upon
Retirement
Get & Keep Your First Job
Get Hired Today
Get into the Right Business School
Get into the Right Law School
Get into the Right Medical School
Get People to Do Things Your Way
Have a Winning Job Interview
Hit the Ground Running in Your
New Job
Hold It All Together When You've
Lost Your Job
Improve Your Study Skills
Jumpstart a Stalled Career

Land a Better Job
Launch Your Career in TV News
Make the Right Career Moves
Market Your College Degree
Move from College into a
Secure Job
Negotiate the Raise You Deserve
Prepare Your Curriculum Vitae
Prepare for College
Run Your Own Home Business
Succeed in Advertising When all
You Have Is Talent
Succeed in College
Succeed in High School
Take Charge of Your Child's Early
Education
Write a Winning Résumé
Write Successful Cover Letters
Write Term Papers & Reports
Write Your College Application Essa

MADE EASY
Cover Letters
Getting a Raise
Job Hunting
Job Interviews
Résumés

OPPORTUNITIES IN
This extensive series provides
detailed information on nearly 150
individual career fields.

RÉSUMÉS FOR
Advertising Careers
Architecture and Related Careers
Banking and Financial Careers
Business Management Careers
College Students &
Recent Graduates
Communications Careers
Education Careers
Engineering Careers
Environmental Careers
Ex-Military Personnel
50+ Job Hunters
Government Careers
Health and Medical Careers
High School Graduates
High Tech Careers
Law Careers
Midcareer Job Changes
Re-Entering the Job Market
Sales and Marketing Careers
Scientific and Technical Careers
Social Service Careers
The First-Time Job Hunter

 VGM Career Horizons
a division of *NTC Publishing Group*
4255 West Touhy Avenue
Lincolnwood, Illinois 60646–1975